Boris Yeltsin

Man of the People

Eleanor H. Ayer

A People in Focus Book

DILLON PRESS
New York

Maxwell Macmillan Canada
Toronto
Maxwell Macmillan International
New York Oxford Singapore Sydney

Photo Credits

Jacket photo courtesy AP—Wide World Photos

AP—Wide World Photos: 6, 35, 53, 56, 68, 79, 82, 91, 98, 101, 107, 110, 111, 121, Sovfoto: 11
Andrew Nurnberg Associates: 13, 19, 20, 29, 47

Dillon Press
Macmillan Publishing Company
866 Third Avenue
New York, NY 10022

Maxwell Macmillan Canada, Inc.
1200 Eglinton Avenue East
Suite 200
Don Mills, Ontario M3C 3N1

Macmillan Publishing Company is part of the Maxwell Communication Group of Companies.

First edition
Printed in the United States of America
10 9 8 7 6 5 4 3 2 1

Library of Congress Cataloging-in-Publication Data

Ayer, Eleanor H.
  Boris Yeltsin: man of the people/by Eleanor H. Ayer. —1st ed.
       p.   cm . — (People in focus series)
  Includes bibliographical references and index.
  Summary: Traces the life of the Russian leader from his childhood on a collective farm through his education as a civil engineer to his election as the first President of the Russian republic in 1991.
    ISBN 0-87518-543-6
    1. Yeltsin, Boris Nikolayevich. 1931- —Juvenile literature.2. Presidents—Russian S.F.S.R.—Biography—Juvenile literature. 3. Politicians—Russian S.F.S.R.—Biography—Juvenile literature. 4. Russian S.F.S.R.——Politics and government—Juvenile literature. [1. Yeltsin, Boris Nikolayevich, 1931- . 2. Presidents—Russian S.F.S.R.] I. Title. II. Series.
DK290.3.Y45A7   1992
947.085'4'092—dc20
[B]   92-16607

Dedication

This book is dedicated to To Russia with Hope, one of many programs started in the United States early in 1992 to help the Russian people make the difficult transition to democracy. Projects like *To Russia with Hope* are people-to-people programs—American people sending Russian people food, medical supplies, and other items to help them through these hard times. If you'd like to be a part of helping the Russian people during this very important period in history, here's how you can get involved:

Write to: The Fund for Democracy and Development
2033 M Street N.W., Suite 506
Washington, DC 20036

You'll receive a newsletter, "Call to Action," which has information about the fund's many programs and an explanation of what your school or community group can do to help.

Acknowledgments

Sincere thanks to Mary Schaeffer Conroy, Associate Professor of History, University of Colorado at Denver, for her careful reading of the text and her perceptive explanations regarding Soviet history and politics.

Grateful appreciation is also extended to Andrew Nurnberg Associates of London for use of selected photos of Boris Yeltsin and his family.

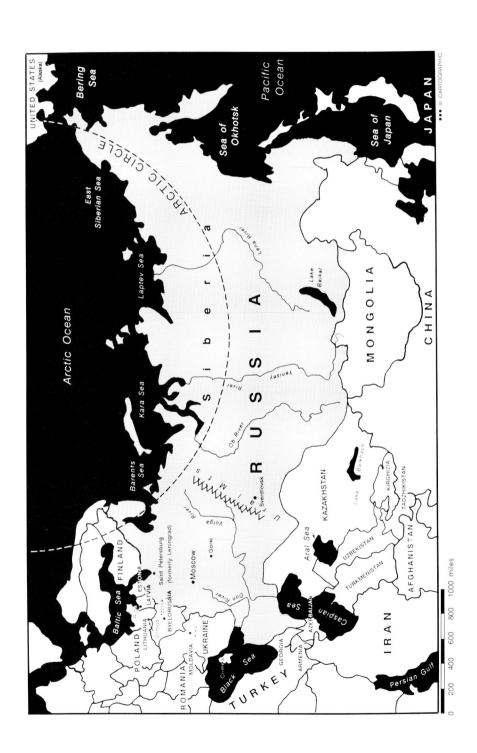

Contents

A victorious Boris Yeltsin and his supporters

Chapter / One

A Fairly Joyless Time

YELT-sin! YELT-sin! YELT-sin! thundered the joyous crowd as its new leader wedged his way to the microphone. It was a day of unimagined triumph, a day that no 20th-century Russian ever expected to see. Never before had the people been able to choose their own president in a free election. Now they had done it. More than half of the Russians who paraded to the polls voted for the man they hoped would lead them out of Communism.

They liked Boris Yeltsin because he listened to them. It was something no Russian ruler had ever done. Not only did Yeltsin listen, he acted. He was not afraid to speak his mind. And if his words ruffled the feathers of Communist Party leaders, well, that was just too bad.

On this day, July 10, 1991, Yeltsin made his first speech as the new Russian President. He told his people that he could not express in words his great feeling of pride and faith. Russian citizens had placed their deepest trust in him, and he promised not to let them down. Leaders should be responsible to their people, Yeltsin believed. "The great Russia is rising from its knees!" he shouted to the cheering crowd. Together, he assured them, they would turn their country into a successful, democratic, peace-loving state, ruled by fair laws. "Russia will revive!"[1] vowed Yeltsin.

He didn't need to tell the people what a precious price they had paid for 74 years of Communist rule. He didn't need to remind them how many of their fellow citizens had died at the hands of tyrants. The names Lenin, Stalin, Khrushchev, Brezhnev, and others were still very fresh in people's minds. They were fresh in Yeltsin's, too, for he had been born into the same oppressive system. His own childhood, he admitted, had been "a fairly joyless time."[2]

That joyless time began on February 1, 1931, in the Russian province of Sverdlovsk. For generations, Yeltsin's family had lived in the little farming village of Butko, scraping out a living from the soil. Raising wheat had never been an easy or rewarding business, but in the early 1930s it was particularly grim. Harvests were poor and food was scarce. This was the world into which Yeltsin was born.

The name Boris was given to him by the village priest. In the little church baptisms were held only once a month. By Russian custom, the baby's parents offered the priest a glass of home-brewed beer or vodka at the ceremony. But by the time little Yeltsin's turn came around late in the afternoon, the priest had already had several glasses. Slipping the baby into the baptismal font, he turned to argue with one of the church members. Yeltsin's mother, realizing her baby had been forgotten, ran to pull him from the water. "Well," remarked the unruffled priest, "if he can survive such an ordeal, it means he's a good, tough lad—and I name him Boris."[3] The name came from a Slavic word meaning "to fight." After that, Yeltsin confessed, religion never played a major role in his life.

What did play a major role was hardship. In the late 1920s, dictator Joseph Stalin and his Communist government began forcing on peasants a new system called collective farming. Under this system the government took control of farms throughout the country. It seized all property except personal items such as clothing and furniture. Peasants were forced to move onto huge collective farms where they worked together to raise crops for the government. Several families lived on each farm, earning barely enough money to keep themselves alive. "The collective farm system proved to be a terrible misfortune," wrote one bitter survivor many years later. "It brought ruin, degradation, and millions of deaths."[4]

Like other peasants, the Yeltsin family was forced to join a collective farm. Fortunately, Boris's father also found work as a construction laborer, helping to build a potash plant. This job kept the family from total, hopeless poverty. The Yeltsins moved from Butko into a communal hut near the farm, the kind the government provided for laborers. The hut had 20 or so small rooms with a hall down the middle. In one of these tiny rooms lived the entire Yeltsin family—Boris, his parents, his younger brother and sister, and the goat that sup-

Making it legal: An offical shows two peasant women the document authorizing the takeover of their private farm. In 1935, when this photo was taken, the women were 100 and 104 years old. They were forced to work on a collective farm.

plied their milk. The six of them slept on the floor, huddled together to keep warm. Outside was the hut's one primitive toilet and the well from which water had to be drawn.

Hauling water was one of Boris's chores, along with watching his younger siblings. The boy knew he had to take good care of the little ones or he would suffer his father's wrath. Boris's father was quick-tempered, like his grandfather, and he blamed his son for whatever went wrong in the neighborhood. No matter if a prank or accident had not been Boris's fault—he was whipped for it all the same. Knowing that it irritated his father when he didn't cry, he did his best to stay dry-eyed during his whippings. Later in life, when he became a father himself, Boris was gentle with his own children, just as his mother had been with him. But like his father, he had a quick temper and a rough, immediate way of speaking his mind.

Boris also inherited his father's interest in new ideas. The elder Yeltsin loved to create plans for new machinery, drawing first in his head, then on paper, then refining and redrawing. His dream project was a machine that would lay bricks, and he was determined to make it work. But such creative thinking and questioning caused him to be hauled from his home late one night by Stalin's terrorist police. Under Stalin, no one was allowed to think for himself or question the way things were. The event was mysterious and terrifying to Boris, then only six. Although his father was eventually returned to the family, that night would mark Boris's memory forever.

This photo, retrieved from an old family album, shows Boris with his parents and younger brother.

For ten tough years, the family lived in the communal hut, Boris and his mother working the collective farm. During the summers, their job was to cut, stack, and prepare the hay for market. They were paid with half the crop; the other half went to the farm. The Yeltsins then sold their hay to buy bread at tremendously high prices, and the next summer the work began all over again.

Despite the family's poverty, Boris and his brother and sister were able to stay in school. He was a good student, if not always well behaved. It was during his graduation from elementary school that his outspokenness first became well known. Some 600 people had gathered for the graduation exercises when Boris asked to make a speech. After thanking some of his better teachers for their work, the boy began a verbal attack on his homeroom teacher. He accused her of mentally crippling and humiliating her students. On and on he went until at last the graduation program ended in disaster, and an irate school board refused to give Boris his diploma.

The incident didn't end there. Boris made sure the government investigated the teacher's conduct, and before long she was dismissed. When, at last, he did receive his diploma, Yeltsin counted it as the first of his many political victories. It was also the first of many times that his outspokenness would get him into trouble.

Boris headed for secondary school despite the turmoil that World War II was then wreaking on Russia. Being too young to join the army, he and his friends decided to make their own weapons, one of them a cannon. It was Boris who volunteered to break into the local church where the ammunition was stored and steal the supplies they would need. Under the eye of a lazy guard, he slipped out with two hand grenades, which the boys carried to a forest 40 miles away to dismantle. Unfortunately, they didn't realize how dangerous it was to take apart a weapon. In the explosion that followed, two of Boris's fingers were destroyed and he was knocked unconscious. Frightened comrades carried him to the hospital, where surgeons removed the useless fingers from his left hand. It had been a close call for Boris Yeltsin—but it wouldn't be the last.

Always the leader, Boris organized annual

summer hikes with his schoolmates. Each trip had a purpose. The boys' mission the summer after ninth grade was to find the source of the Yaiva River, high in the Ural Mountains. A few days into the expedition, the group ran out of food, but they forged ahead, living off berries and plants they found in the woods. The trip took much longer than they expected, but at last they found the object of their search—a natural spring. Mission accomplished, they rested a bit and gathered their strength to head home.

It was the return trip that nearly brought disaster. So tired were the boys from the first half of their journey that they decided to find a boat to carry them home. In a remote village, they traded what few possessions they had for a flat-bottomed craft, and headed back. A short way into the trip, they stopped to explore a cave and the hills around it. Had they not taken this side trip, the expedition might have ended safely. But soon they became lost and wandered for nearly a week in the wilderness without food or fresh water. At last, desperately thirsty, they drank some stagnant water from a small pond, which made them extremely ill. Being the expedition leader, Boris felt responsible for finding the way back. Even though he was as gravely ill as his friends, he carried each of them to the boat and laid them in the bottom. Somehow he got the group home, where a doctor diagnosed their high fevers as typhoid, a deadly disease. For months, all were wretchedly ill. Most of the group missed the entire tenth-grade year. But about midterm, Boris began studying at home, for he had a goal in mind. The following year, he wanted to start college.

Perhaps because his father was a construction worker, Boris set his sights on studying civil engineering. But before he could take the tests to enter the Urals Polytechnic Institute, his grandfather insisted that he build something with his own hands. It was to be a bathhouse, a luxury the family had never had, and Boris was to build it from scratch. Grandfather made certain that Boris drew the plans, cut and hauled the trees for the lumber, and did all the building himself. During the weeks of work that followed, the old gent never showed his face. But when the project was completed, he gave it a thorough inspection—and his approval.

Building that bathhouse helped him more, Boris said, than all the hours of studying for the Polytechnic entrance exams.

Learning how to build bridges, highways, and large buildings was most interesting to Boris. So were sports. Always a competitive athlete, his aim was to play every sport and play it well. Not long after entering the Polytechnic, he became president of the sports association, in charge of organizing all sporting events for the school. His own specialty was volleyball, which he played nearly six hours a day, in competitions that took him all over the Soviet Union.

If he wanted to play ball, Boris realized, he must study very late at night and early in the morning. This schedule left him only three to four hours for sleep, but it was a habit that stayed with him all his life. He learned to work hard and continuously with very little rest.

It was his love of volleyball, Boris admitted, that "all but brought me to the grave."[5] During exam time, because of his exhausting schedule, he contracted tonsillitis and a high fever. Still he refused to stop training. At last one day, his heart pounding and sweat soaking his body, he collapsed

At the Polytechnic, Boris coached the women's volleyball team.

on the volleyball court and was rushed to the hospital. Doctors told him that if he stayed in bed at least four months, he might avoid permanent damage to his heart. But a few days later, with the help of some friends and a rope made of bed sheets, Boris lowered himself from a top-floor hospital window and headed home. Soon he was back on the volleyball court, beginning with one minute of training a day, then two, then five. By the end of a month he could play a full game. "I had taken a colossal risk," Yeltsin later wrote, "but it paid off."[6]

This was not the only colossal risk Boris Yeltsin would take in his life. And it was not the only time his friends would come to his aid. In fact,

A *playful* Boris (*behind the guitar player*) *with friends from the* Polytechnic.

such close friends did the Polytechnic students become that they made plans to meet every five years for a reunion. To this day, they keep that promise, sometimes bringing their families, and usually heading into the wilderness. One year they hiked in the Urals; another, they organized a sailing expedition to an island in the Arctic Ocean. Through the years, their friendship has grown even closer. "Whenever I [have] found myself in difficult situations," Yeltsin says of his Polytechnic pals, "they have responded by offering me their support. One can safely say that these are real friends."[7]

Chapter / Two

A Severe Reprimand

Brushes with death had become a part of Boris Yeltsin's life. It wasn't that he was careless or foolhardy—he was curious and competitive. He simply could not resist a new challenge. Never content with his accomplishments, Boris continually looked for ways to better himself.

This desire to improve led him to a job as a dump-truck driver after he graduated from Polytechnic. Despite excellent grades in school, Yeltsin felt unprepared to take a job in civil engineering. He knew complex mathematical formulas and theories, but he couldn't lay bricks or drive a crane. So he said "no" to becoming boss of a construction crew and decided instead to spend a year learning the building trades. If he were going to be in charge of other workers, he wanted to know each man's job firsthand.

Boris worked for a month as a mason, then for a month as a carpenter—one month at 12 different trades for a full year. It was during his month in concrete mixing and pouring that he defied death once again. The dump truck he was driving was very old, and his load of liquid concrete was extremely heavy. Unfortunately for Boris, the old clunker picked a railroad crossing on which to stall. To his horror, he heard a train bearing down on him from a distance, moving toward him at a high speed. He could open his door and jump, but that would be irresponsible. Besides, he had no money with which the replace the truck. As the train rushed nearer, he frantically recalled that if he pushed the starter, the truck would lurch forward a little. Over and over he pounded that starter until, at last, the hulk inched off the tracks. Seconds later the train shot by, leaving a weak and breathless Yeltsin sitting by the side of the road.

Some people might have considered this brush with death enough work for one day. But not Boris. After finally getting the cantankerous truck to start, he delivered the load of concrete to the construction site. Leaving a job undone or doing it in a slipshod way were habits Boris Yeltsin would not condone. "Good, professional, high-quality work never goes unnoticed," he maintained. "If you've given your word, keep it—you must answer for it."[1] This dedication to doing a job and doing it right helped to make Yeltsin a leader.

After spending a year in the building trades, Boris believed he was ready to run a construction crew. As foreman, he directed workers in the building of factories, machine shops, concrete plants, workshops, and schools. He soon discovered that knowing how to manage his workers was as important as being able to do the job himself.

On one of his first projects, he headed a crew of convicts. Yeltsin felt that these men were overpaid, so he lowered their earnings to what he thought they were worth. When the workers got their next paychecks, they were angry. The leader of the group, a big man, showed up at Boris's office, an ax in his hand. He was already a convict, he sneeringly reminded his boss, so he had nothing to lose by swinging this ax at him. Demanding the former rate of pay for himself and his fellow workers, the giant screamed at Yeltsin, "I'll smash your skull before you've even had time to squeak."[2]

Realizing it was useless to fight back, Boris decided on a different approach. Making his voice as deep and resonant as he could in the small office, he roared at the convict, "Get out!" Somewhat to Yeltsin's amazement, the giant dropped his ax and meekly left the room. This was not the style of management that Boris Yeltsin preferred, but sometimes it was necessary.

What he did prefer was to set a good example for his workers. He liked to show them just what he expected and encourage them to work up to the same high standards that he set for himself. On every job, he tried to work harder than anyone else. His greatest strengths included "my own total dedication to the job, my insistence on high standards . . . plus people's faith in the rightness of what I was doing."[3]

He always tried to get to know his workers. Understanding their concerns would, he believed, make him a better manager. If his workers felt that he cared about them, they would do a better job for him. He put these ideas to work while he was chief engineer on a housing project that employed several thousand people. Boris showed up to work the night shift with a crew of women who were finishing the interior decoration of a building. Rolling up his sleeves, he plunged into wallpapering and painting window frames while he chatted with the ladies about their jobs and families. Learning that they'd like mirrors in the dressing room at work, Boris saw that it was done. From time to time after his visits, dress material or other gifts would arrive for the women, as thanks for having done a good job. These little things helped to build better bridges between Boris and his employees.

Yeltsin worked well with women. His own wife, Naya Girina, helped to tame his rough, outgoing manner with her gentle ways. Naya and Boris had met when they were students at the Polytechnic in the 1950s. Although they had fallen deeply in love during their second year in school, both kept very busy schedules. Boris was often away on tour with the volleyball team, which left little time for them to be together. After graduation, under the Communist system, students were assigned by the government to work in certain areas. Boris was told to stay in Sverdlovsk, but Naya was sent back to her home province of Orenburg. Using this separation as a test of their love, they decided to meet in a year to see if their feelings were still the same.

That was the year Boris spent learning the building trades while playing volleyball on the city team. Toward the end of the year, the team toured in Naya's town. The two met and, realizing nothing had changed, decided at once to get married. At that time in the Soviet Union, people could marry on a moment's notice, without having to register in advance with the government. The young couple went to the marriage bureau, where an official performed the ceremony. In earlier years, Boris had organized many friends' wedding receptions. Now some 150 of those friends from around the country gathered for a party that lasted all night.

It was a fine marriage, if not an easy one. Nearly four decades later, Boris would admit that life with him could get tough at times, being "obstinate and prickly" as he was. But, he added, "I need hardly say that I have always loved Naya—and will love her all my life."[4]

After their marriage, Naya went to work for the Institute of Waterways, a job she would hold for 29 years. Soon, their first child, daughter Lena, was born. Although he was overjoyed at the birth, Boris had to confess he had wanted a boy. Immediately, he began trying old wives' tales, like putting an ax and a man's peaked cap under the pillow, to insure that the next child would be a boy. Despite his efforts, daughter Tanya was born two years later. Little Tanya was like her mother—kind and soft-spoken; Lena, her father admitted, was more like himself.

Most of the child care fell onto Naya's shoulders, for Boris was away much of the time. Still, father and daughters got along well, and the girls always tried to please him. He set high standards for them and expected them to do well in school. A grade of 80, he told Lena and Tanya, "was not a mark worth getting."[5]

When the girls were very young, Boris and Naya vacationed by themselves. But as the children got older, the whole family took camping trips into the wilderness. "Those were real vacations," Yeltsin wrote many years later, when he was a government leader. "There was nothing but laughter from morning till night, for we kept inventing funny games and quizzes and playing practical jokes. One could totally relax."[6]

But as Boris grew more involved in his work, there were fewer carefree days. By the late 1950s, he had been named chief engineer of all construction projects for his region. His new job with the government brought him into much closer contact

Boris always had a close relationship with his daughters. Here he embraces Tanya.

with Communist Party leaders, although he was not yet a Party member himself.

For years, Yeltsin had studied Communist thoughts and ideas. He knew that while the Party had full control of the government, only 6 percent of the Soviet citizens actually were members. Millions of lives were controlled by a very small group of people, and Boris Yeltsin wanted a voice in that control. At last, he decided the time had come to apply for Party membership.

Immediately, he hit the first of many roadblocks that would haunt his political life. An important Party official with whom Boris had once disagreed now tried to block his membership. In the interview required of all applicants, the man asked Yeltsin some questions about the writings of Karl Marx, the 19th-century German philosopher considered one of the fathers of Communism. In which volume and on what page of *Das Kapital*, Marx's famous book on economics, did he write about commodity-money relationships? the accountant demanded. Boris had no idea. But immediately he answered, "Volume Two, page 387." He was guessing his interviewer knew less than he did about the writings of Karl Marx—and he was right. "Well done," his questioner admitted. "You know your Marx well." Boris's bluff had worked.

But the very day after receiving his Party membership, he also received a "severe reprimand."[7] His scolding came from the City Committee, a local Communist Party group. They were using Boris as an example to teach other Party members a lesson. Just a few weeks earlier, Yeltsin had become head of construction on a boarding school project. The person he replaced was known for his poor workmanship and drinking habits, and thus the school was very far behind schedule. Although there was no hope of completing the job on time, the City Committee still gave Yeltsin a bad report, which went on his permanent record.

It came as a "serious blow," Boris admitted. He had joined the Party because he believed in its ideas of fairness and justice. As a new member, he planned to give the Party his full support. "And then suddenly this had to happen. . . ."[8] Over the years, Yeltsin would discover many more problems within the Communist Party. But for the time being, he was still a believer.

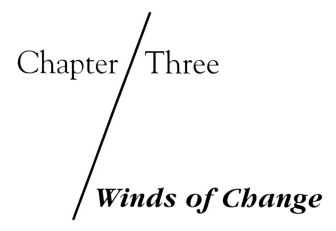

Chapter / Three

Winds of Change

Boris Yeltsin's road to political success was paved
with giant boulders. His outspoken manner and his
habit of questioning rules and authority did not
make him popular with Communist leaders. They
wanted "yes-men" who would quietly do what they
were told in exchange for benefits to themselves
and their families. Yeltsin was not that type of person. Nevertheless, he became more and more
involved in politics and spent long hours working
for the Party.

Boris's new interest in government was inspir-
ing him to "make a move in a new direction."[1] For
14 years, he had been a civil engineer, a career he
very much enjoyed. He had a good reputation for
performing high-quality work on time. Now he was

ready for a change, but he wasn't sure just where the change would take him. Fate answered his question when the Party asked him to head its office of construction in his home province of Sverdlovsk. Thinking this was a good chance to move ahead, Boris accepted the offer.

In his new position, he kept his usual high working standards. "I drove myself harder than anyone else."[2] And although many could not keep his pace, Boris didn't push them beyond their limits as he did himself. He just wanted his workers to try their hardest. Yeltsin's high standards paid off, and soon he became Secretary of the Construction Committee.

As one of several Party secretaries, Boris was sent to Moscow, the Soviet capital, in the fall of 1976 to study for two weeks. Much to his surprise, a few days into his stay, he was told to report to the Central Committee. This was a group of 400 top members of the Communist Party Congress. Why in the world the Central Committee wanted to see him, Boris could not imagine. He met with one person after another until at last he was told to report to the Kremlin, the offices of the most important officials in the Soviet Union. There, he was told, he would meet with Leonid Brezhnev, President of the USSR.

A very nervous Boris entered the plush offices, an escort at his side. "So," Brezhnev began, speaking to the escort, "he's decided to assume power in Sverdlovsk Province, has he?"[3] The aide explained that Yeltsin as yet had no idea what was happening. Only then was he told that his name had been suggested over several other higher-ranking leaders to become First Secretary of his province. This meant a big jump forward in the Party. Quite surprised at the offer, Boris stammered that he would "do the job to the very best of my ability."[4]

As First Secretary, Boris Yeltsin was the most powerful person in Sverdlovsk Province. It was his job to work with Party leaders in Moscow to coordinate food supplies, arrange for large construction projects, and help factory managers in their operations. The last word on all major decisions for the province was his. This power was intoxicating, Yeltsin admitted. Yet he promised to use his position only for the improvement of his people.

He began at once to get to know the folks he represented. Sverdlovsk Province was made up of 45 towns and 63 smaller communities. He planned

He made it a point to get to know the people he represented.

to visit each one at least every two years. It was important to him to know not only the leaders, but the ordinary people as well. Often he and Naya made the trips together on a working vacation.

In many towns, he arranged meetings in which groups of students or workers could ask questions, tell him their concerns, or offer ideas for changes. This was a first. Such gatherings were simply unheard of in the USSR. Party leaders never encouraged people to complain or ask questions. If citizens were unhappy, they didn't want to hear about it.

Yeltsin knew that millions of citizens *were* unhappy. For years, the Communist Party had promised them a perfect world, where everyone was equal. Party leaders would create this perfect world by controlling the nation's economy. The government would decide where people should work, how much they would be paid, what goods they would produce, and what prices would be charged for those goods. Everyone would have an equal chance to buy food, cars, and household appliances. The government would see that every family had a place to live. There would be no rich or poor; each person would work for the good of all citizens—not to make more money for himself.

But after more than half a century of Communism, people saw that the system wasn't working the way they had been promised. Instead of the perfect world, masses of people lived near poverty. Their lives were bleak and gray, with no hope for improvement. Under President Leonid Brezhnev, the government was making no progress in improving the way people lived. Yeltsin called it "the Brezhnev 'era of stagnation.'"[5] Party leaders used their positions to improve their own lives, but gave little thought to the common people. Brezhnev, being a very weak president, was powerless to stop the corruption around him.

Boris believed that Brezhnev had "no idea what he was doing, signing, or saying."[6] The President's aides, Yeltsin claimed, had all the power, and they were using it to their own benefit. The common people had been forgotten. "The system," Yeltsin cried, "was clearly beginning to fail."[7]

To make his voice heard, Boris realized he needed some contacts on the powerful Central Committee—those top 400 men in the Communist Party Congress. But he knew very few people on the Committee. At last, in 1978, an acquaintance of his, Mikhail Gorbachev, was elected Secretary of the Central Committee for Agriculture. This connection might prove helpful, Boris imagined. Little did he know what effect his relationship with Mikhail Gorbachev would one day have on the world.

Before his election to the Central Committee, Gorbachev had been First Secretary of the

Stavropol Province, at the same time Yeltsin was First Secretary in Sverdlovsk. The two had talked on the phone and arranged for the trading of food and raw materials between their provinces. They got along well. At that time, Boris recalled, Gorbachev was "more open and frank."[8]

For a time, their relationship continued to go smoothly. The first sign of conflict came when members of the Central Committee filed a report about Yeltsin. The group had visited Sverdlovsk Province and reported a number of good points as well as bad in the way the province was run. Boris accepted both. But he stressed to the Committee that the report contained some errors. Members were shocked. Good Party men simply did not mention mistakes in their bosses' reports.

Immediately, Boris was ordered to a meeting in Moscow to face Party leaders. He met with several before finally being called by Gorbachev. "You should draw the necessary conclusions!" his former friend barked at him. Yeltsin wasn't quite sure what he meant. He told Gorbachev he had studied the report but that he was not going to make any changes because of the errors it contained. Gorbachev stood firm: "You're wrong,"[9] he warned.

It was the first real run-in between the two men, and it would not be the last. For several years, Gorbachev was a far more powerful figure in the Communist Party than Boris Yeltsin. But this didn't stop Boris from speaking his mind. He was finding it harder and harder to keep quiet about the corruption he saw everywhere within the Party.

Building a better life for his people was becoming Boris's greatest goal. To gain the power needed to achieve that goal, he knew he had to build a good relationship with the Soviet military. Just as he had done when he headed construction crews, Boris made it a point to visit personally with the soldiers. He joined them in their training, learned how to operate their equipment, and listened to their problems and concerns. At first, they were afraid to be frank with him. But when they realized they would not be hurt by speaking out, they talked much more freely. Yeltsin was pleased; he saw this greater openness as a good sign among his people.

He also improved his relations with the KGB, the Soviet Union's secret police and intelligence agency. Although many of the agency's activities were carefully concealed, Boris educated himself as completely as he could. His knowledge of the KGB proved very helpful to him as he continued to climb the Communist Party ladder.

For nine years, Yeltsin served as First Secretary of Sverdlovsk Province. During that time, he worked hard to improve the living conditions of his people. He set a number of tough goals for himself and didn't quit until he reached them. One of his goals had been to get rid of the deplorable wooden huts he remembered from his childhood. Millions of Soviet citizens still lived in these communal shacks. Since the government was in charge of building new housing, Boris believed Party leaders should correct the problem. He proposed a plan. For one year, only people who lived in the huts would be allowed to move. All housing money for that year would be put into building new homes for them. Yeltsin knew this would make him unpopular with factory managers. He would be using the money that managers needed to build housing for their own workers and spending it instead on the hut dwellers. The managers did protest, but Boris held firm. No one, he insisted, should "have to live in such conditions in the twentieth century."[10] Boris got his way, and the hut dwellers got their new homes.

It was an important victory. Yet what Yeltsin considered his greatest success during his term as First Secretary was the building of the 220-mile Sverdlovsk-Serov highway. Before this road was built, the only transportation through the region was a ten-day trip by train. The highway cut that time down to a few hours, but construction conditions were terrible. The route ran over the worst possible terrain—mountains, rivers, swamps, ravines, and bogs. The new road, as expensive and difficult as it was to build, did open the province to easier access and more business, which greatly helped the people of Sverdlovsk.

Throughout his term as First Secretary, Boris put every ounce of energy into his work, trying always to do his best. Yet over the months, he became more frustrated and less satisfied with his job. It was getting increasingly tough to accomplish projects because the government moved like molasses. Not only were agencies slow to act, but they rarely provided enough funding to do a job right. Much of the money seemed to be going straight into the pockets of Party bigwigs.

Yeltsin was also becoming frustrated by the attitude of Communist Party leaders. He had known when he joined that he would have to follow orders. But he was not prepared for the "pressure, threats, and coercion"[11] that he often faced on a job. Leaders were very good at making people do what the Party wanted. They were masters at offering suggestions people didn't dare to refuse. And though he didn't know it, Yeltsin was about to become the next target of their coercion.

Chapter / Four

The Move to Moscow

It wasn't a move he wanted to make. Boris would have preferred to stay right in Sverdlovsk, the place of his birth. This was his homeland and he loved it. Sverdlovsk was where his friends and supporters lived. To outsiders, Moscow seemed like a city of stuck-up snobs. It was the Soviet Union's showcase city, displaying the best that the USSR had to offer—good meats, fancy shoes, items the people of other provinces hadn't seen in their own stores for years. Moscow was where you went to get an education, to get ahead, to become successful. But the real down-to-earth people, the good common folk, lived in places like Sverdlovsk—or so Boris thought.

When the first call came, asking him to

become head of construction on the Central Committee in Moscow, he said "no" at once. There
were many reasons why he didn't want the job.
Most important was his reluctance to leave
Sverdlovsk. The people, his work, his accomplishments as First Secretary—all were too important to
leave behind him.

There was another reason. Sverdlovsk was the
third largest industrial province in the Russian
Republic, an area of nearly five million people.
Boris's nine years as First Secretary of the province
had given him much valuable experience. His position was one of importance and influence. The
new job would be a comedown, and Boris knew it.

When the second call came, it was more
demanding than the first. This time it was from
Yegor Kuzmich Ligachev, the number-two man in
the Communist Party. Of course Comrade Yeltsin
would be taking the new position, Ligachev
insisted smugly. He reminded the reluctant Yeltsin
that, as a Communist Party member, he was "obli-
gated to accept the [job] and move to Moscow."[1]

Boris was being coerced, and he didn't like it.
But neither was he ready to give up his position in
the Communist Party. Sadly, and against his better

judgment, he said good-bye to Sverdlovsk and made the move to Moscow. He began his new job and life in the big city on April 12, 1985.

Depressed and uninterested, Boris took the first apartment he saw, in a dingy, dirty section of the city. Only the challenge of a new job with much work to be done kept his spirits alive. Here in Moscow, working amid the highest-ranking Party members, he no longer had the authority he had had in Sverdlovsk. For years Yeltsin had been top dog, used to making all his own decisions. Now he had to go through channels to get permission and answers. The pace was slow and the frustration intense.

Daughter Tanya had moved to Moscow earlier, so Boris did have some company as he began his new career. Soon Naya arrived, along with Lena, her husband, and their two daughters. It was good to have his family with him, but Boris found that he had less time for them than he had had in Sverdlovsk, and this bothered him.

Despite the discomforts, he threw himself into the new job with his usual zeal. Soon he found it was not the comedown he had thought it would be. By June, he had been elected a secretary of the

Central Committee, in charge of the country's entire construction business. While this position may have sounded important, Boris saw it as nothing more than the next logical step up the political ladder—a job that a man of his experience had earned honestly.

With the new position came a new house—a *dacha*, or country house. These homes were reserved for important government officials. Mikhail Gorbachev and his wife, Raisa, were just moving out as the Yeltsins were moving in. Now that he had become General Secretary of the Central Committee—the most powerful position in the Communist Party—Gorbachev had been given a nicer home.

Unlike the Yeltsins, Mikhail and Raisa enjoyed the good life—beautiful homes, new cars, expensive clothing. Fancy houses were unimportant to Boris and Naya. They preferred a simpler way of living, like the people they represented. This difference in life-style would one day become a major point of disagreement between the two leaders.

Not only did the Yeltsins reject a fancy lifestyle, but Boris began speaking out against Party leaders who did chase the good life. He considered

Yeltsin with wife Naya, daughter Tanya, and grandson Boris

it decadent and irresponsible for leaders to live so much more elegantly than the people they represented. Why should a Party official's bill from an expensive restaurant be paid by the government when thousands of common citizens were going hungry? Boris demanded. He got no answer.

Deciding he could remain silent no longer, he vowed to expose the culprits. It was nearly impossible. How could he bring bribery, corruption, and misuse of government money to the attention of Party leaders when they were the very ones to blame? He met with Gorbachev to discuss his concerns, but the General Secretary refused to believe him. Yeltsin was wrong, Gorbachev insisted; there was no such corruption in the government. But Boris persisted until, at last, Gorbachev lost his temper and dismissed him from the meeting.

Despite his outspoken ways, Yeltsin kept his place in the Party. On December 22, 1985, he received a summons to attend a meeting of the Politburo, a small, select group of leaders chosen from the Central Committee. Gorbachev headed the meeting, and he came right to the point. The Politburo, he said, wanted Yeltsin to become chairman of the Moscow City Committee of the Communist Party. This committee, made up of 1.2 million members, was in trouble as a result of poor management, the Politburo reported.

Boris knew that Viktor Grishin, then head of the City Committee, was a man of "no great intellect," and that he "lacked any sense of moral decency." Grishin had no concern for the common people; he simply used his office for his own personal gain. Thanks to Grishin, life in Moscow was "worse than it had been several decades before,"[2] Boris believed. The city was dirtier, there were endless lines, and public transportation was overcrowded. The Politburo wanted to force Grishin out, and it planned to use Yeltsin as its lever.

When Boris protested, saying he was not the right person for the job, the Politburo reminded him that he had an obligation to the Party. It didn't matter that he preferred to stay in his current job. If he could be of greater service to the Party as head of the Moscow City Committee, then that was what he must do.

It was coercion again. On December 24, still wondering why Gorbachev had suggested him, Yeltsin took over his new position. Grishin was gone, but his men were still there, and Boris's first job was to remove them. He needed to surround himself with people he could trust, people who would work with him to bring changes both in Moscow and around the country. From top to bottom, Boris selected a whole new staff, much to the irritation of many Party members, who saw his choices as liberal thinkers who were threats to the system.

But the people welcomed these liberal thinkers. After years of being afraid to speak out, even in private, they were ready for the freedom of speech that Boris Yeltsin encouraged. Greater openness—*glasnost* the Soviets called it—was gaining strength around the country. People were tired of the heavy hand of government threatening their every thought and act.

Certain members of the Supreme Soviet—the upper house of the Soviet Congress—knew in their hearts that *glasnost* was the way of the future. But few were ready to risk their secure jobs, nice homes, and new cars to support it. Mikhail Gorbachev was one of the few. He knew that if *glasnost* were to become a way of life in the Soviet Union, the government had to be restructured. Greater openness and honesty would mean a change in the old dictatorial Communist system.

Gorbachev called his restructuring plan *perestroika*, and he wrote a book explaining his ideas. There would be greater separation between the government and the Communist Party. No longer would groups like the Supreme Soviet be rubber-stamp bodies that automatically approved whatever the Party proposed. The government would be allowed to question the Party's ideas. Gorbachev's plan made him a hero around the world. Never before in a Communist country had leaders talked of ideas that might go against the Party. Gorbachev was doing it. But at the same time he was trying to show his comrades that he was still "a good Party man who thought good Party thoughts."[3]

Yeltsin supported *perestroika*. He was delighted with the changes in government that restructuring brought. He was overjoyed by the positive feeling of hope that was beginning to creep into the country. But he was not pleased with the snail's pace at which Gorbachev's economic reforms seemed to be moving. What Yeltsin wanted was "concrete results and some steps forward."[4] He wanted to see greater changes in the economy—the way money and goods were produced and distributed—in the USSR. Unless they saw action, he feared, people would soon tire of the fancy phrases and grand promises about *perestroika*.

In an effort to promote greater openness and clean up corruption within the system, Boris went to the offices of the newspapers *Moscow Pravda* and *Moscow Komsomol*. He talked with editors and writers, encouraging them to publish stories that exposed crime and wrongdoing in the city. Moscow television got the same green light. Boris assured the reporters that by keeping quiet about problems, they weren't helping to heal them. They were merely "covering them up with sweet-smelling cream so they wouldn't be visible."[5] Delighted with this new freedom, the press plunged into its work and soon drew fire from hard-line Party members, those who resisted change. But Boris defended the reporters, saying they were helping him to clean up the Soviet capital.

Transportation was also high on his list of ill-nesses to cure. Hearing that many workers had long, crowded commutes into Moscow every day, Boris decided to see for himself. Early one morning, he boarded a bus in one of the suburbs, transferred

Yeltsin talks with foreign reporters and cameramen.

to a subway, and rode an hour and a quarter to Moscow with thousands of other commuters. On other routes he found the same slow, overcrowded conditions.

Becoming a commuter not only helped him understand the city's transportation problems, but it also gave him a chance to talk with the people. Yeltsin encouraged groups to meet with him and ask questions. He tackled the toughest issues and tried always to supply answers.

When someone suggested there might be corruption in the management of certain grocery stores, Boris began an investigation. At first, most workers didn't want to tell what they knew for fear of losing their jobs or homes. But one woman's disgust with the system overcame her fear, and she decided to talk. She told Yeltsin about store clerks who were ordered to overcharge their customers. At the end of each day, the "extra" was given to the boss, who passed it out among the top managers. The woman's confession led Yeltsin's staff to investigate hundreds of stores, and within a year, some 800 workers and managers had been caught.

Despite his efforts to expose corruption and promote truth, progress was not happening fast enough for Boris. He did not keep quiet about his concerns. At meetings of the Politburo, he spoke out about the slowness with which change was coming to the Soviet Union. He had faith in Gorbachev, Yeltsin assured Politburo members. But he felt it was time to restructure even the highest levels of government. And he wasn't sure Gorbachev was willing or able to challenge Party leaders who might stand in his way. Although aware of his rival's feelings, Gorbachev did little to quiet him.

On February 18, 1986, Yeltsin himself became a candidate member of the Politburo. This group, headed by Gorbachev, was the real center of power in the Communist Party. It was a move upward for Boris, and he never quite understood why he was promoted. "I sometimes wonder," he wrote, "how I managed to end up among all these people." It was hard for Boris to believe that a system designed to choose only good "yes-men" could have "failed so badly as to choose Yeltsin."[6]

The rookie spent his early weeks studying the structure of the meetings and trying to educate himself on issues he thought members would discuss. "At first," he recalled, "the emptiness of our sessions was not so noticeable."

But as he became more familiar with the meetings, he realized that what the members were doing "was often pointless."[7] There was much talk but little action. Gorbachev held a blind belief that *perestroika* would somehow sweep the country. Boris accused him of living in a dream.

Instead of a grand new era of openness and restructuring of government, he saw a new era of stagnation and do-nothingness creeping in, just as it had in Brezhnev's time. There was plenty of talk but few improvements in the lives of Soviet citizens. In his usual forthright fashion, Boris Yeltsin set a new goal. He would light a fire under *perestroika*, the Politburo, and the Communist Party. The fire might, in the end, destroy him, but at least he would have brought some action and change into the stagnating system.

Yeltsin continues to speak out against corruption.

Chapter / Five

The Yeltsin Affair

A bulldozer. That's what people were calling Boris Yeltsin. As he churned and plowed his way toward the top of Soviet politics, he made as many enemies as he did friends. Even those who liked him agreed that Boris was not a tactful person. In fact, said one, "His lack of tact was probably his undoing." Boris's supporters called him "colorful"; Gorbachev called him "overzealous and impatient."[1] Some people called him worse than that.

Whether you loved him or hated him, Boris Yeltsin was not a man to be taken lightly. Among the *apparat*, a group of powerful politicians he called a "huge, lumbering machine,"[2] Yeltsin made many enemies. The *apparat* included most of the Central Committee. These hard-liners were afraid of losing their jobs and their luxurious life-styles. They would listen to talk of *perestroika* and *glasnost*—as long as it went nowhere. But Yeltsin's efforts toward reform gave them cold feet. And when he spoke about a free, democratic society, they could barely bring themselves to listen.

Yeltsin, for his part, was becoming more and more disgusted with the "perks" and privileges granted to Party officials. He refused to travel like the rest of them, in a ZIL limousine, the fancy Russian car provided to Party bigwigs. Instead, Boris rode public transportation with his fellow Muscovites.

He was upset by Party leaders who did little to modernize their towns, factories, transportation and communication systems. These leaders seemed content to let their people live in the past, without modern appliances or technology. He was irritated by the special treatment that Party bosses received in department stores. Certain sections of the stores were set aside for Party leaders only; no common citizens allowed. Here the nicest products were sold, but only important officials could buy them.

The same applied to hospitals. Some wings were reserved solely for treating high-ranking Party members. VIPs were given rooms by themselves or with one other person, while the common folk had to crowd 10 or 12 patients into a room. The way Yeltsin saw it, Communist Party leaders were enjoying the good life while millions of Soviet citizens lived near poverty.

He continued to speak out against corruption, but he could see that he was running up against the massive brick wall of the *apparat*. Relations with members of the Politburo were getting worse, he admitted, "no doubt owing to my difficult character."[3] Yeltsin's criticism of the slowness of change was also getting him into trouble. So far, Gorbachev had put up with his outspokenness. But the General Secretary was beginning to lose patience with the man he had once called a trusted ally.

One of the *apparat* with whom Yeltsin clashed most was his old enemy Ligachev, who was then in charge of the Central Committee. The two disagreed on everything from Party perks to *perestroika*, and they argued fiercely during Politburo sessions. One big issue was the sale of liquor. Ligachev had decided it was time to wipe out alcoholism in the Soviet Union, so he issued an order forbidding the sale of liquor. Yeltsin was in favor of trying to cut down alcoholism, but this plan struck him as ridiculous. People would not stop drinking, he predicted, just because they couldn't buy alcohol. They would find illegal ways to buy it on the black market. The sale of vodka brought much money into the Soviet economy. If gangsters started selling it, they would get the money instead of the government. Yeltsin protested that because Ligachev had not given the plan proper thought, it was doomed to fail.

After several months, the anti-alcohol program did fail. Yet Ligachev maintained it was working well, and because he was a high Party official, people believed him. Finally in frustration, Boris requested a meeting with Gorbachev. For more than two hours, they talked about Ligachev and a long list of other concerns. Gorbachev listened and seemed to understand why Boris was upset. But he cautioned him to wait, have patience, give things a chance to correct themselves.

Boris wasn't willing to wait. The others could continue their middle-of-the road, do-nothing ways, but this route was not for him. Feeling trapped in political quicksand, Boris decided to make a bold, brash move—a move that meant almost certain suicide for a rising politician. He asked to be relieved of his duties; he wanted to quit his job.

Boris began his resignation letter of September 12, 1987, by telling Gorbachev how difficult this decision was for him. At first, he admitted, he had seen some chances for success in his new job. But after 19 months as a candidate member of the Politburo, he confessed that his "personal sense of dissatisfaction has only increased." The letter mentioned the change in other Party members' attitudes toward him, how the feeling of "friendly support" had turned to one of "indifference" and "coldness."[4] He spoke of his conflicts with Ligachev, his frustration with the pace of *perestroika*, his distrust of Party members who were afraid to speak their minds. "I am an awkward person," Boris admitted, adding that he did not want his awkwardness or strained relations with his comrades to hurt Gorbachev's work. Therefore, the letter concluded, "I wish you to release me from the duties of first secretary of the Moscow City Committee . . . and from my responsibilities as the candidate member of the Politburo."[5]

As he sealed the envelope, Boris wondered if

he were doing the right thing. Nevertheless, he had it delivered. After several days, Gorbachev called to suggest that they meet later. It seemed Yeltsin's request was not going to be heard until the plenum—the quarterly meeting of a small group of leaders from the Central Committee.

Then and there Boris decided to speak at the plenum. Immediately, he began bracing himself for what might take place. He knew the meeting would be a rehearsal of speeches that officials planned for the 70th anniversary of the October Revolution. This was the event that had first brought the Communists to power in 1917. The speeches would condemn Communist tyrants like Stalin, who had ruled the USSR with a murderously brutal hand for nearly 30 years. Then the tone would turn to the amazing accomplishments of current leaders and the positive progress of *perestroika*. It would be a time for Party officials to pat one another on the back and compliment one another on their successes. Yeltsin knew that the speech he planned would blow a blast of cold air over the meeting.

As he walked into the plenum on the day of his speech, he was having second thoughts. Should he ruin the mood of the meeting by going into a tirade about the present government? Or should he wait to give his speech until the anniversary had passed? This speech could, Boris knew, be the final nail in his political coffin. Central Committee members would probably be glad to accept his resignation and shove him out the door. What he planned to say was not what these people wanted to hear. While Gorbachev finished the rehearsal of his anniversary speech, Yeltsin wrestled with his conscience. But he knew what he had to do. He had to tell the Politburo exactly what was on his mind.

Sensing what was about to happen, Ligachev, who was running the meeting, now tried everything in his power to keep Boris from speaking. It was Gorbachev who finally insisted that his rival be allowed to address the Committee. Yeltsin came right to the point. Despite two years of positive talk about *perestroika*, very little had been done. "People's faith," he warned, had begun "to ebb."[6] Citizens were losing respect for the Party. Common people simply didn't see Gorbachev as the hero the Politburo tried to make him. The people wanted a leader who would take action, Yeltsin advised, not a politician who made vague promises. He ended his attack on the government by asking once more to be released from his duties.

Later, as he reflected upon his speech, Yeltsin wondered "whether I really needed to have charged in as I did, guns blazing; to have caused the uproar that resulted in such a drastic change in my life." But no amount of soul-searching ever caused him to regret his act. "The speech I made then was indeed necessary,"[7] he maintained months later, although he did admit that it might have been poorly timed.

As he ended his address, a series of attacks followed on the plenum floor. Some two dozen speakers took the platform, one by one, to criticize Yeltsin and his speech. It was as bad as Boris had imagined—and worse. Even Eduard Shevardnadze, the Soviet foreign minister who would later be his supporter, now turned against him to defend Ligachev. Gorbachev accused him of putting his own concerns ahead of the Party's. "I consider this an irresponsible action,"[8] he scolded Boris. Still the Politburo did not dismiss him. Instead, he was given one last chance to speak.

Realizing that it was useless to criticize, Yeltsin

decided to be humble. In his final remarks, he explained that his attack on the government had been caused by his great desire to improve the quality of life in the Soviet Union. Speaking quietly but firmly, he apologized for his unlimited ambition, his great love of action and progress. He admitted that he had tried to control this ambition, but without success. "I am very guilty before the . . . Politburo and certainly before Mikhail Sergeyevich Gorbachev."[9]

The whole affair was too much strain for the man some called "emotional, proud, and extremely vain." Boris's mental and physical health began to fail, and within days he was in the hospital. Officials warned that he was too sick to be disturbed, even by his own family. Yet on the third day of his stay, he received a phone call from Gorbachev asking him to attend a meeting of the Moscow City Committee that very day. Yeltsin was stunned. Surely this was the end of his political career, yet never had he known of anyone "being dragged out of a hospital bed to be dismissed."[10]

Still he went. So full of sedatives was he as he entered the City Committee meeting that he claims to have understood "practically nothing of what was happening around me." It was a lynch scene, "like a real murder,"[11] Yeltsin later wrote. Gorbachev led the lynching, claiming that no one on the Central Committee supported Yeltsin anymore—a statement that was not true. He defended Yeltsin's right to speak out, but in a qualified way, saying that criticism was fine, as long as a person didn't disagree with his comrades. (But why would anyone criticize if he didn't disagree?)

Finally, after defending *perestroika* one last time, Gorbachev turned the meeting over to the Committee. One by one the members ripped and tore at Boris Yeltsin's character. They called him "a demagogue, a dictator," and "altogether incompetent."[12] Through his haze of medication, Boris listened to them rave on and on against him. At last, mercifully, the Committee accepted his resignation. Still in a stupor, he dragged himself to a waiting car for his return to the hospital.

These events clearly showed that *glasnost* had its limits. In the Soviet Union, people still could not speak their minds without fear of punishment. Even Gorbachev would later admit that the Yeltsin Affair, as it would be known, was a setback to progress. The next day Soviet papers—particularly *Pravda*, the official newspaper of the Communist Party—printed only criticism of Yeltsin. There were no details of his speech at the plenum. The Communist press wanted the Soviet people to see Boris as a rabble-rouser. The rest of the world, however, saw him as a victim. The inhuman way in which he was treated, said one American writer, reminded him of "pre-*glasnost*, even of Stalinist" days.[13]

The Russian people were outraged by the way Yeltsin was being treated. A well-known chemist, who just weeks earlier had praised *glasnost* and *perestroika*, now said, "I'm no longer optimistic. . . . Something has changed inside Gorbachev."[14] Students took to the streets in Moscow, holding pictures of Yeltsin and demanding that Communist newspapers print his side of the story.

In spite of this support, Boris Yeltsin was reaching a low ebb in his life. Many of those who had spoken out against him were people he had thought were his friends. "I found it extremely hard to bear their betrayal."[15] His heart, he said, was "a burned-out cinder."[16]

*As Party hard-liners attacked Yeltsin, average citizens demon-
strated on his behalf.*

In trying to pick up the pieces of his life,
Yeltsin looked to himself for strength. Some people, he knew, turned to God in times of crisis, and
some to a bottle of liquor. But neither of these
methods worked for Boris. His family gave him
great support, despite his very bad moods, feelings
of guilt, and periods of depression. For this, he
would always be grateful. During his long hours in

the hospital, he analyzed himself, his personality, and his relationships with people.

There were even rumors that he was contemplating suicide, which Boris found ridiculous. "I am not like that; my character will not allow me to give in."[17] Never, he said, would he have taken such a step. What he needed was time to rebuild his own strong character, time to reassure himself that he was still a good person, acting in the ways he thought were right. "It was a time of fierce struggle," he recalled. "I knew that if I lost that fight, my whole life was lost. The tension within me was extreme."[18]

Chapter / Six

A Born-Again Politician

It seemed as though Gorbachev just wouldn't let up. As Boris lay in his hospital bed, trying to rebuild his life, another phone call came from government headquarters. Why couldn't they leave a beaten man alone? Then, to Yeltsin's utter astonishment, he realized that the General Secretary was calling to offer him a job! Would Yeltsin consider becoming First Deputy Chairman of State Construction? Gorbachev wanted to know.

It was amazing. Why would the man who had just helped to murder him politically suddenly want him back in the government? Was Gorbachev worried that the Yeltsin Affair had given him a bad reputation? Was this job a way to keep Yeltsin in politics without giving him too much power?

Boris could find no reason for this mysterious move. Finally he decided that, in some strange sort of way, Mikhail Gorbachev needed him. He needed a "prickly, sharp-tongued" bad boy in the Party, a radical who would make the rest of the *apparat* look good. "It is my belief," wrote Boris, "that if Gorbachev didn't have a Yeltsin he would have had to invent one."[1]

Not really caring *why* he had been offered the job, Boris said "yes," he would take it. He would enjoy being back in civil engineering. In his new position, he would be working for the Soviet government, not for the Party, as he did when he was head of construction for the Central Committee. Within days he was out of the hospital and back on his feet.

As the new head of all government construction, Boris threw himself into his work with his usual enthusiasm, but it wasn't easy. He was still looked upon politically as a dead man. Criticisms continued to be hurled against him. Now, more than ever, he was an outcast—an oddball among high-ranking Party members. Few were willing to stand up for him publicly. Those who did were primarily friends from his Polytechnic years.

Now that he was back in construction, he had little contact with Gorbachev. During the next year and a half, they met only once. Still, Yeltsin felt that "the ice was breaking up" between them. He began, cautiously, to think that a political comeback might be possible. "New times were on the way," Boris recalled, "in which I had to find a place for myself."[2] It would mean rebuilding his career from the beginning, but he was willing to try.

Being a deputy chairman made him eligible to be chosen as a delegate to the Nineteenth Party Conference. This was a group of 5,000 people picked from the Communist Party to represent all republics of the USSR and other Communist countries around the world. Elections to the June 1988 conference would be held soon, and Boris saw this as a good time to begin his political rebirth. Groups from Moscow and Sverdlovsk tried to get him elected as a delegate from their regions, but each time, the *apparat* blocked his election. At last, just in the nick of time, he was chosen as a delegate from Karelia, a small region where the *apparat* probably figured he would have little voice.

With his foot now back in the political door, Yeltsin set his next goal: to be a speaker at the conference. Although his past outspokenness had nearly killed him politically, he had no intention of keeping quiet. Early in the conference, he requested a chance to speak, but by the last day permission had not been granted.

Frustrated once again, Boris decided to "take the rostrum by storm." The 5,000 people gathered in the hall watched uneasily as he marched toward the platform, "looking Gorbachev right in the eye."[3] There were whispers and rumblings as Central Committee members discussed whether or not to let Yeltsin take the floor. At last, after much deliberation, Gorbachev announced that Yeltsin could speak.

"Comrade delegates!" he began, and quickly plunged into a discussion of all the problems currently facing the Party. There was *perestroika*, there was the issue of free election of officials. And what about *glasnost*—just how much openness was possible in a Communist society? He mentioned "forbidden, secret topics such as the details of the party's budget,"[4] and matters of social justice. Yeltsin spoke on and on until at last he came to what he called "a ticklish matter."[5]

The ticklish matter was his rebirth as a politician. He asked the conference delegates to withdraw his resignation, which they had accepted at the October 1987 plenum. If they chose to bring him back, Yeltsin promised, it would "help the cause of *perestroika* by increasing . . . confidence in the Party."[6]

Noisy discussion erupted in the hall, and Boris offered to sit down. But Gorbachev told him to go on. "I think we should stop treating the Yeltsin Affair as a secret,"[7] the General Secretary confessed. When his speech was over, Boris returned to his seat amid applause, and the conference adjourned for lunch.

When the meeting resumed, Boris's opponents took the floor. One by one, he recalled, they "diligently showered me with mud,"[8] until it began to look as though his chance for a political rebirth was hopeless. Only one person, a delegate from Sverdlovsk, came forward to say a word in his support. The rest of his allies were afraid to defend him in public. As the criticism went on, tension mounted in the hall. Boris began to feel ill, as if he were "on fire inside, and everything was swimming in front of my eyes."[9] This constant barrage of fiery criticism was destroying his soul and spirit.

At last the attacks stopped, and conference delegates began discussing the issues before them. They settled their regular business, but no suggestion was made to restore Boris as a politician. The issue was never even raised. Feeling extremely sick in body, mind, and heart, Boris left. It looked now as if he surely would remain a dead man in the Communist Party.

In the end, the press was able to do what the conference delegates would not. For the first time in history, thanks to *glasnost*, the June '88 conference had been televised. Millions of Soviet citizens had heard Yeltsin's speech. They had seen him attacked by Ligachev and others, and they didn't like what they saw. The public was outraged by the way Boris Yeltsin had been treated.

The publicity made him a hero among the common people. They wrote him long letters, suggesting everything from massage to raspberry jam to help him rebuild his strength. "In sending me those encouraging letters they were holding out their hands to me," Yeltsin wrote, "and I was able to lean on them to get on my feet again."[10] It was this support that, over several long weeks, brought Boris back to health. So what if the *apparat* refused to allow his political rebirth? He had the support of the people, and they were voicing their opinions loudly and strongly.

Mikhail Gorbachev heard them, and what he heard moved him to make some changes. By September 1988, the General Secretary was doing things he had promised the *apparat* he never would do—like restructuring the Communist Party. Hard-line Party members were suddenly out the door. Some were fired; others resigned in the face of Gorbachev's sweeping changes. Ligachev, Yeltsin's old rival and the number-two man in the Party, now found himself in a much less important position. It seemed that, at last, Gorbachev was heeding Yeltsin's warning—that *perestroika* could not succeed with the *apparat* in power.

As the door swung shut on Ligachev and other old-line Communists, it opened again for Boris Yeltsin. By December, his political comeback was on a roll, and he knew what he had to do next. His plan was to get elected to the Congress of People's Deputies, a group like a parliament, made up of 2,250 members from around the country. Election to this congress would give him the chance to rise higher in the government. But now the election was just three months away, and Boris and his supporters had much work to do.

Yeltsin knew he faced tremendous obstacles in winning this election. The first hurdle was to get his name on the ballot, a move that the *apparat* would try to block. Gorbachev had made many strides toward ridding the top government of those resisting change, but enough hard-liners still remained to make life miserable for Boris Yeltsin.

Knowing that he could count on support from his home region, Boris headed back to Berezniki, a town in Sverdlovsk. By early January 1989, he had accomplished his goal of getting on the ballot there. But being elected from Berezniki would be only a small victory from a small town. It would mean much more if he could get elected from Moscow. Boris decided to try. He would keep his name on the ballot from Berezniki just in case; but he would use the next weeks to try to outsmart the *apparat* in Moscow and get on the ballot there.

The Party bigwigs were as determined to keep Yeltsin off the ballot as he was to get on. As part of their effort to silence him, they published a ten-page booklet of reasons why Yeltsin should not be considered as a candidate. The booklet claimed that "injured pride, ambition . . . and a lust for power"[11] were what had prompted him to run. These latest slams hit Boris very hard, even though he knew he shouldn't take them seriously. "It is high time I learned to react calmly," he wrote. "But I can't!"[12]

Despite these and other roadblocks, Yeltsin finally found success. On February 21, he was accepted as a candidate from Moscow. With only one month remaining before elections, Boris took to the streets. He made sure his face appeared all over the city, for now, he figured, was when his opponents would mount their strongest campaign against him. Surprisingly, the *apparat* remained fairly quiet. Even an "investigation" into Boris's character, launched by the Central Committee just ten days before the election, failed to discredit him. It was becoming obvious to everyone that Yeltsin had the strong support of the people and that their voices would carry him to victory.

Just how great a victory, not even Yeltsin himself could have imagined. When the results of the March 26 election were counted, he had received an astonishing 89.6 percent of the vote! In the first free elections since 1917, some 5.1 million people

Trying to make a comeback, Yeltsin campaigned all over Moscow.

had voted for Boris Yeltsin. He was by far the most popular politician in Moscow.

The election fires had barely cooled when, a couple of months later, people started saying that Yeltsin would challenge Gorbachev, who had just become President of the USSR. But Boris quickly denied such plans, claiming that he supported Gorbachev's policies for the moment. What he wanted next was to be elected to the Supreme Soviet, the upper house of the Congress of People's Deputies, made up of 542 officials. The Supreme Soviet had recently been restructured, and its new members paid more attention to the affairs of the country than the old delegates had. The group met twice a year, for three to four months each time, to make and explain the laws.

Once again Yeltsin was a long-shot candidate. Members of the Supreme Soviet were chosen by the Congress, and Boris knew his chances of being picked by these politicians were slim. As he sat through the meeting, watching other, more qualified candidates go unpicked, he knew he would never win. The *apparat* seemed finally to have had enough of Boris Yeltsin.

When he wasn't chosen, the people at home went wild. They had followed the meeting on television, and they didn't like what they had seen. They wanted Yeltsin in the Supreme Soviet, and so did many of his fellow deputies. The people accused Gorbachev and the rest of the Congress of slipping back into Stalinist days.

Suddenly, Yeltsin found himself aided by an unexpected ally. A lawyer from Siberia, Alexei Kazannik, one of the deputies just chosen to the Supreme Soviet, now offered to resign—but only if Yeltsin could take his place. Gorbachev didn't know what to do. Finally, he decided that the only way he could keep the respect of the people was to agree. And with that, Boris Yeltsin became a member of the Supreme Soviet.

The people of Moscow were delighted. As Yeltsin left the meeting to walk home, "hundreds of Muscovites flocked around him, pumping his hand and handing up babies to be kissed."[13] Not only had he been reborn politically, Boris Yeltsin was fast becoming the most popular politician in the USSR.

The people felt that Boris was a leader they could believe in.

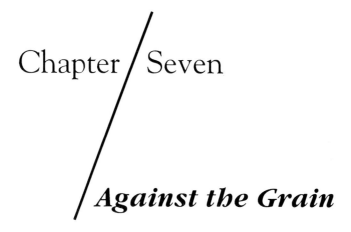

Chapter / Seven

Against the Grain

What made Boris Yeltsin so popular with the Soviet people? He was a leader they felt they could trust, a person who understood their frustrations and concerns. He seemed to be one of them. Unlike other Communist Party officials, he didn't live a life of luxury while the common people suffered. He cared about their suffering and he listened to their problems.

Yeltsin knew that Soviet citizens were fed up with the Communist government. They were tired of standing in long lines to buy food—*when* there was any food to buy. In recent years, mistakes in government planning had left more and more grocery shelves bare. The wait to buy a car or a household appliance could be years. In desperation, many had turned to the black market—an illegal route to getting what they wanted, usually at high prices. Crime was on the rise, and it was no secret that Party chiefs were growing richer while the common man grew poorer. People were reaching their boiling points, and Boris Yeltsin understood their frustration.

Yeltsin now had some solid plans for pushing *perestroika* at a faster pace. He wanted to change laws about ownership and use of land. He wanted to set limits on the powers of the Communist Party. He wanted greater freedom of the press. He wanted less money spent on defense and government construction. But Gorbachev wasn't willing to give him the go-ahead on these new ideas.

There were others in Congress who were. One by one, Party members began speaking out against the pace of *perestroika*. But they knew that unless they banded together as a group, their voice would never be heard. The *apparat* would see that as individuals they were kept quiet. So it was that, in spite of Gorbachev's warnings against starting subgroups within the Congress, Yeltsin and his radical comrades organized the IRGD.

The Inter-Regional Group of Deputies wanted

private individuals and companies—not the government—to own the land. "Only when the land is
worked by the people who own it will the country
be fed,"[1] the IRGD believed.

Private ownership of land would take away
power from the central government, which was
another goal of the IRGD. This group wanted to
give more power to the governments of the 15
republics that made up the Soviet Union. Reduc-
ing the power of the vast central government
would allow the republics to raise and spend money
as they thought best. Closer control of the money
would, the IRGD hoped, strengthen the Soviet
economy. This must happen soon, they knew, or
the ruble (the unit of Soviet money) would
become worthless.

The sick society had other problems that the
IRGD hoped to correct. The USSR was made up of
many different groups of people—among them,
Russians, Armenians, Moldavians, Ukrainians, and
Jews. Ethnic rivalries and hatreds had existed long
before the Communists came to power in 1917.
Indeed, only the strong arm of the Soviet central
government had managed to keep violent clashes
from breaking out. The Communists had not, how-

ever, taught the people to be tolerant. Only the
threat of military force had suppressed the ancient
animosities. Now, as the central government was
losing its iron grip and the individual republics
were asserting their strong national feelings,
Yeltsin—and others—feared for the safety of the
people.

Although he was not particularly religious
himself, Yeltsin wanted the church to become
stronger. For years, the Communist government
had controlled the church and worked to downplay
its importance among the people. Now it was necessary, Yeltsin thought, for the church to rise and
help bring an end to the hatred and strife that were
beginning to break out again.

By the end of June 1989, the IRGD's voice was
being heard in the Supreme Soviet. Some of the
most intelligent people in the country made up this
group. Yeltsin learned a lot from them. They taught
him to analyze, to weigh and balance all sides of an
issue before speaking his mind. He learned "not to
be so harsh and intolerant and coarse in his expres-
sions."

And how did the intellectuals see Yeltsin?
"Like a big child, rather naive," said one. But most

admitted that they were "won over by his sincerity."[2] Still, he scared many of them. From history they had learned that a national hero can quickly become a dictator. When a country is going through hard times and its citizens are unhappy, it is easy for a dictator to grab power. He promises the people what they want: an end to their problems. All they have to do is follow his rules without question. Because intellectuals do question authority and prefer to think for themselves, they are not often popular with dictators. The IRGD worried that Yeltsin might be another Stalin or Hitler.

There were others who thought Yeltsin was too rough around the edges to become a prominent world leader. He simply wasn't smooth and polished enough to present a good public image. These people found proof for their fears during Yeltsin's September 1989 trip to the United States. Several American groups had invited him. They wanted to get to know this man who was defying the Soviet system. According to Yeltsin, the trip was supposed to take two weeks, but at the last minute, the Central Committee decided he could leave for only one.

This change of schedule, he claimed, was the

cause of his troubles on the American visit. Trying to cram into one week a tour that included eleven cities, several speeches, and a meeting with President George Bush was simply too much. Although Boris blamed his behavior on his exhausting schedule, certain members of the American press saw things differently. Some reporters claimed he was drunk, not exhausted. The *Washington Post* reported that he drank a large quantity of alcohol during his stop in Baltimore, Maryland. So unsteady was his walk, the story said, that he looked like a circus bear on a skateboard.[3]

Back home, *Pravda*, the powerful Party newspaper, said Yeltsin had been "hopelessly drunk."[4] *Pravda's* report, based on a story in an Italian newspaper, sent Yeltsin into a rage. Most of the money he had earned by giving speeches on his American trip he had donated to fighting AIDS in the USSR. Yet *Pravda* claimed he had spent it on expensive clothing, videos, and other fancy American goods. Boris called the attacks against him "stupid and bold-faced lies."[5] Once again his faithful followers rallied behind him. The thousands of telegrams they sent in support were proof of Yeltsin's popularity.

Blessedly for Boris, the scandal died down as

world events heated up. One after another, the Communist/Socialist countries of Europe began declaring their repressive governments to be dead. In November, Germany's 28-year-old Berlin Wall—the symbol of Communism that had divided free West Berlin from Communist East Berlin—came crumbling down along with East Germany's Communist government. It hurt Yeltsin to see how fast these changes were sweeping other countries while *perestroika* dragged along in the USSR.

The Supreme Soviet had just gone back into session, and it looked once again as if members would do little to change the old ways. Yeltsin lashed out at the group, calling it "Gorbachevian." Just like its chairman, he said, the Supreme Soviet was "constantly lagging behind the march of events." He accused Gorbachev of being timid and called him a lover of "half-measures and semidecisions."[6]

Those close to the capital were now beginning to hear political rumblings that scared them. There was talk of an uprising to remove Gorbachev from power. Yeltsin considered these reports the wildest kind of gossip, but he promised to fight for Gorbachev if it became necessary.

Why would he defend a man with whom he so

often disagreed? Because Boris believed that without Gorbachev the country would fall into chaos. Civil wars would erupt; thousands would die. Although he felt that his boss's beliefs would one day "be his downfall," Yeltsin knew that right now Gorbachev was "the only man who [could] stop the . . . collapse of the Party.[7] And at the moment, Yeltsin didn't want the Party to collapse.

You see, he was not against Communism itself; he was against the beliefs and ideas that current members of the Communist Party held. Boris wanted to clean up the Party, to bring in some fresh faces, some people committed to action and change.

But by the time the Twenty-eighth Party Congress met in July 1990, it was clear that there was little hope for change. Neither was there any more time to wait. The Party's long-held grip on the Soviet Union had "reduced the country to a desperate condition and the people, tens of millions of them, to poverty."[8] If conditions did not improve, Boris warned, the Party was doomed and so was the country.

At last, seeing no hope left for the Communist Party, Boris Yeltsin decided on a drastic move. He quit. Yeltsin chose the Party Congress meeting to

Despite their differences, Yeltsin supported Gorbachev for the sake of the nation.

announce his decision. Waiting until members had nominated him to the new Central Committee, he stood up and broke the news to his fellow congressmen. "Stunned former comrades watched in silence,"[9] one writer reported. A few Central Committee members yelled "Shame!" as Yeltsin left the meeting, but some of his supporters quit as well. Although he was nervous and sleepless for many nights, Boris never regretted his move. It was, he later said, like being freed from a false religion. For the first time in its history, the USSR now had a major political figure who was not a member of the Communist Party.

Chapter / Eight

A Burning Convert to Democracy

Boris Yeltsin's good-bye to the Communist Party was just one of many cracks appearing in the Soviet Union's foundation. Rumblings of independence were growing louder among the 15 republics. They wanted to rule themselves rather than be ruled by the central government of the USSR. Yeltsin supported independence for the republics, but he was not yet ready to dissolve the USSR. There should be some union, he believed, some thread to tie the republics together.

Yeltsin and Gorbachev disagreed about independence. Gorbachev wanted a strong central government; Yeltsin wanted independent republics. Yet, strangely, this disagreement brought them closer together, for both were fighting to keep some sort of union. Neither wanted to see the USSR dissolve into 15 separate countries with no common head.

Without a central government, who would control the Soviet military and the vast store of nuclear weapons held by the USSR? Would each republic have to raise its own army and navy? Some of the republics were rich in natural resources, while others grew huge amounts of food. Without some kind of union, it would be difficult for each republic to supply all the needs of its people.

For some time, the three Baltic republics— Estonia, Latvia, and Lithuania—had been moving toward independence. Finally, on January 13, 1991, the rumblings erupted into violence. In the Lithuanian capital of Vilnius, Soviet soldiers stormed a television tower, killing 13 citizens who were trying to protect it. There were rumors that the attack had been ordered by Gorbachev, that this was his way of crushing independence in the republics. But Gorbachev claimed the attack was a complete surprise to him.

Yeltsin flew to Lithuania, right into the middle of the crisis. He spoke out loudly in support of the republic and its drive for independence. Not surprisingly, his actions turned the anger of the Soviet army against him and led to a bitter argument with Gorbachev. Over the next few months, each man would try to force the other out of office.

Still, the Soviet President knew that he couldn't push Yeltsin too far, for Yeltsin held the key to keeping the Soviet Union alive. Russia, with its 147 million people—more than half the country's population—was the largest and most powerful of the Soviet republics. This region was rich in natural resources, providing nearly 90 percent of all the oil and natural gas shipped from the USSR. Both leaders realized that "without Russia there could be no Soviet Union at all."[1]

It was a tricky position for Gorbachev. He had to handle Yeltsin in just the right way or he risked losing a major chunk of his empire. And handling Boris Yeltsin was getting tougher and tougher. He was now considered the most popular politician in Russia, which made it hard for Gorbachev to criticize him. To make matters worse, since he quit the Communist Party, Yeltsin was fast becoming a "burning convert to democracy."[2] For many years, he had studied democratic governments. He had seen them work in the United States, in Japan, in

West Germany. He had watched the year before as the Communist countries of eastern Europe made painful but positive changes toward democracy. Yeltsin wanted these changes in his own country. He wanted a government that would give his people the freedom to vote as they wished, live where they wanted, and improve their lives to the best of their abilities.

The first step toward democracy, Yeltsin believed, was independence for the 15 republics. What stood in the way was Gorbachev. In a television interview, Yeltsin called *perestroika* a failure and Gorbachev a dictator. He had tried, he said, to cooperate with the President. But he could see that Gorbachev was not willing to allow independence in the republics. Then, in a statement that sent shock waves around the world, Boris Yeltsin called upon Mikhail Gorbachev to resign.

Many people, including some of his own supporters, were upset by Boris's demand. Some journalists and political leaders suggested that his judgments were not always sound. Others said he was making no more progress toward changing the country than had Gorbachev. "People are losing hope,"[3] one teacher sighed. Even Yeltsin himself was beginning to lose hope. "I feel burdened, tired, and drained by this totally senseless conflict,"[4] he complained.

Nevertheless, Yeltsin's daring and dangerous move did pay off. A few days later, 100,000 Muscovites rallied in the streets shouting, "Yeltsin, president—Gorbachev, leave." They demanded that Gorbachev turn over his power to the leaders of the 15 republics. The President refused to resign, but with public opinion so much against him, he at last began to cooperate with his old rival.

"Yeltsin for President" signs now began appearing all across the Russian republic, where a presidential election was coming up in June. The people demanded a chance to vote for the candidate of their choice. If the people got their way, it would be a first. They had been allowed to vote in other elections, but never to elect their own President directly.

In April, the Congress of People's Deputies said "yes." It would allow the election of a Russian president by a direct vote of the people. In May, the Supreme Soviet and the Congress approved final details of the election. With the date set for June 12, candidates now had just three weeks to campaign. Yeltsin knew his toughest competition would be the Communist Party candidate, and he was right. Immediately, Party rivals began doing everything they could to put Yeltsin down. They called him a buffoon and a lightweight. An article in *Pravda* said he was "disloyal, unpredictable . . . and incompetent."[5] The story claimed Yeltsin had a great need for power but could not handle stress. By now, Boris was used to such attacks. When asked what he would do if he lost the election, he told reporters, "I shall retire and go and dig my garden."[6]

But there was no need to get out the gardening tools. When the election was over and the votes were counted, more than half were for Boris Yeltsin, the first freely elected President of the Russian Republic. It was a tremendous victory— and a severe blow to the Communist Party. Although he claimed not to believe this himself, many people now said Yeltsin was the most important man in the Soviet Union, more powerful than Mikhail Gorbachev. With Gorbachev losing strength, Soviet citizens now wondered how long the USSR could survive.

World leaders like George Bush wondered the same thing, but the American president still had

Yeltsin supporters wave banners saying "We Got the Upper Hand" after the first free election of a Russian president.

the greatest respect for Gorbachev. Despite the upheavals taking place in the Soviet Union, Bush said he would continue to do business primarily with Gorbachev.

Nevertheless, shortly after his election, Yeltsin scheduled a trip to the United States. This time he was received much more politely than he had been in 1989. The drunken bear on the skateboard was seen now as the powerful leader of a reborn nation.

Boris liked Americans. After his first trip, he had decided that they were "surprisingly open, sincere, and kind people." During his entire visit, he said, he could not remember meeting "a single person who was grumpy or sad."[7]

American audiences seemed just as interested in what Boris was saying as the folks back home did. This attitude pleased and surprised him. But what Yeltsin had to tell them was not good news. At a meeting with American reporters, he admitted that he saw no hope for the survival of the Soviet Union. There was no way, he said, speaking of Gorbachev, that one man could preserve the unity of the country any longer.

Very hard times lay ahead. Early in 1991, 100,000 coal miners had gone on strike for higher pay. Without coal, five of the country's huge steel mills had to close. Now more miners were threatening to strike, which could affect another major Soviet industry—oil.

Selling oil to foreign countries usually brought huge amounts of money into the USSR. But with coal miners on strike and machinery breaking down, it looked as if 1991 exports would be only half of what they had been the year before.

To make matters worse, the fuel shortages

forced factories to reduce production. Already the government had raised the cost of many goods, and it looked as if prices would go up again.

With less oil and gas to run their equipment, farmers hadn't planted as many crops. What they did raise, they had trouble storing and shipping. The result was a shortage of food. But food wasn't the only thing that was getting short—so were people's tempers. They wanted change, and they wanted it *now*. Yeltsin knew that as President of Russia it was up to him to make those changes in his republic. But he was quick to warn his people that things would get worse—much worse—before they got better. There were no "quick fixes"; the change would be long and painful.

The IRGD plan of turning over government-owned farms and businesses to private individuals and companies now became one of Yeltsin's major goals. The companies and farmers—not the government—would set the prices of goods. This would be the first step toward a free economy and, Yeltsin hoped, a better life for the people. Competition among companies would give citizens a greater choice of products and prices. It would motivate people to work harder and produce finer

On a visit to the United States, Yeltsin is amazed at the selection of foods in a grocery store—a strong contrast to the food shortage in Russia.

products. In the long run, privately owned businesses would strengthen the nation.

But in the short run, the change to privately owned companies would hurt. Businesspeople would need time, money, and experience before they could develop successful companies. For years, the government had kept prices low on many goods. Prices would skyrocket when government controls were removed. These changes would take a while; the people would have to be patient.

But time was running out. When people are hungry and unemployed, they cannot be patient.

Boris Yeltsin knew this. He was gambling that he could hold the Russian republic together long enough for these new programs to show some promise of hope. In time, he knew, a free economy and a democratic government could make his nation a world leader. But one big question haunted him: *Was* there enough time? Could—and would—the people wait for these positive changes to happen?

Chapter / Nine

The 1991 Russian Revolution

Mikhail Gorbachev's star was fading fast. The leader whom *Time* magazine had named "Man of the Decade" in 1989 was now scrambling to save his country and his job. Daggers were being hurled at him from all sides. He was under constant attack from Boris Yeltsin. His popularity with the Soviet people had reached new lows. And he was rapidly losing favor with his own Communist Party.

In the minds of many Party members, Gorbachev was caving in to Yeltsin's democratic movement. He was now leaning toward giving greater power to the individual republics. In fact, he was trying to pass a treaty that would strengthen the republics and leave the central government very weak. Communist Party members saw Gorbachev's treaty as the last straw. If it passed, it would spell the end of the USSR.

Faithful members knew that the Party was teetering on the edge of disaster. One Russian writer compared it to an airplane "hurtling through the air without its wings and about to crash." Was there any way to keep the plane from crashing? Many thought the answer was to get rid of Gorbachev. Some took that idea one step further. "As soon as Gorbachev is removed, Yeltsin will be destroyed immediately,"[1] the same Russian writer predicted. With those two gone, the Party would once again have a tight grip on the central government.

So what were they thinking, these last loyal members of the *apparat*? They were thinking coup—a lightning quick move to grab back the power that Gorbachev had let slip away. By overthrowing Gorbachev, they could save the Communist Party, preserve the old Soviet Union, and put an end to this upstart Boris Yeltsin. It was risky, but it was the Communists' last chance. And it had to be done before August 20, 1991, the day set for the signing of Gorbachev's treaty.

Unfortunately for the organizers of the coup, nothing went the way they had planned. In fact, when it was over, people wondered if they had really planned at all. It was a botched-up mess from the beginning.

Events started on Sunday afternoon, August 18. Mikhail Gorbachev was vacationing at his *dacha*, 900 miles south of Moscow, working on the speech he would deliver at the treaty signing. Suddenly, there was a knock on his office door. An aide announced that a group of important people were there to see him. Since he was not expecting any visitors, the Soviet leader decided to make a call before admitting them. But when he picked up his phone, it was dead. Gorbachev knew he was in trouble. Immediately, he called his family together and told them to expect the worst.

When he returned to his office, the "visitors" were waiting for him. To his astonishment, Gorbachev recognized five of his most trusted friends. But they were not there on a friendly mission. Immediately, they demanded that he sign a statement saying the country was in a crisis, a state of emergency. The coup plotters planned "to bring discipline back to daily life."[2] All Gorbachev had to do was admit that a state of emergency existed; the coup group would take care of the "discipline."

If he refused to sign, they warned, he must immediately turn over all power to his Vice President, Gennadi Yanayev.

Gorbachev laughed bitterly at both options and told the men to get out. Shaken by his refusal to sign, the coup planners did leave, but not for long. Early Monday morning, the Soviet news agency *TASS* reported that Gorbachev was ill and had turned over power to his Vice President. It was a lie, but it stunned the world and propelled Boris Yeltsin into action.

When Yeltsin first heard the news, he was furious. One thought dominated all others in his mind: Mikhail Gorbachev must be returned to power immediately. It was up to him, Boris knew, to come to the aid of his old rival. At once, he and his staff left for Moscow, 12 miles away. The trip could have been very risky if the coup plotters had planned things right. They could have captured Boris Yeltsin along the way. But they didn't, and Yeltsin remained free to fight the coup.

Boris's group headed straight for the Russian parliament building, a big white marble structure known as the "White House." From here Yeltsin would rally the Russian people to fight the coup. At 11:00 A.M. Monday, he called a press confer-

Yeltsin on top of a tank outside the Russian "White House," urging the people to stand against the coup.

ence with reporters from around the world. When asked if he were worried about being captured, he replied, "I will never be removed [from my office] by anyone except the Russian people."[3]

Shortly after noon, Boris climbed on top of a tank outside the White House to speak to a small crowd of Soviet citizens. He called the coup illegal and challenged the people to fight it. As word of Yeltsin's appearance spread, the crowd grew from a few hundred people to tens of thousands. His aides passed out an appeal "To the Citizens of Russia," a paper encouraging them to go on strike and to demand to see Gorbachev on television.

The crowd caught Yeltsin's fighting spirit. As Soviet troops descended on the city, Muscovites stopped them in the streets. Fearless people placed themselves in front of huge tanks and implored the drivers to turn around. They begged the military men not to fire on their fellow citizens, but it was hardly necessary. The troops supported the people. When asked if he planned to shoot at the crowds, one soldier replied, "Are you crazy? My mother's out there."[4]

Later that day, Yeltsin sent a message to Gennadi Yanayev, the man who had proclaimed himself the new Soviet President. "Keep in mind that we do not accept your gang of bandits,"[5] Yeltsin warned. But the coup plotters didn't need a warning. By now, Yanayev and his men knew that they had made a fatal mistake by failing to capture Boris Yeltsin.

At noon on Tuesday, 150,000 people gathered for a demonstration in front of the White House. Yeltsin was there to speak. "We will hold out as long as we have to," he assured them, "to remove this junta [the coup group] from power."[6]

Rumors began to spread that coup leaders would attack the White House in the early morning hours on Wednesday. To protect Yeltsin and his aides working inside, citizens began building barricades and forming human chains to circle the building.

Many of the people were teenagers like 14-year-old Andrei Vishilovski. "I came here to defend Russia," he said. "I had to do this."[7] Why did Andrei and thousands of Russian teens want to be here? "We're hoping to find ourselves in the future," explained 17-year-old Yevgeni Schistokov. "We're hoping now there will be a future."[8] Boris Yeltsin had shown these young people that they could turn against the old Communist system and change the face of their nation. They were ready to fight for their leader and for a better future for themselves.

At the urging of his staff, Yeltsin now declared all army units stationed in the Russian Republic to be under his command. But would military leaders disobey orders and listen to him instead of Yanayev? After all, the military still belonged to the Soviet government, not to Russia. Later that night, Boris had his answer. As a unit of tanks entered the city, the commander ordered his men to move through Moscow toward the White House. But they were not moving in to attack; they were coming to protect Boris Yeltsin and the Russ-

Tank driver Nikolai Amelin, one of the first soldiers to come over to Yeltsin's side.

ian people. The general in charge of the tanks and armored trucks near the barricades told his men to turn their guns away from the White House and to carry no ammunition. There would be no firing on Yeltsin's headquarters.

By Wednesday, it was clear that the coup was failing. All through the rainy night, crowds camped outside the white marble building, ready to fight if necessary. It wasn't necessary. Except for one encounter—a misunderstanding that left three people dead—there was no fighting.

By afternoon, Yeltsin's Defense Ministry had ordered military troops to leave Moscow. As tanks

The coup defeated, Yeltsin proudly waves the flag of Russia.

and trucks rolled out of town, many proudly flew the white, blue, and red flag of Russia, not the red and yellow hammer and sickle of the Soviet Union. The message was clear—these troops now defended Russia, not the Union of Soviet Socialist Republics.

At 2:15 A.M. on Thursday, Mikhail Gorbachev returned to Moscow. His safety was still in danger; many feared that the plotters would try to kill him in a last desperate attempt to save the Communist Party. But instead, most members of the coup group were running for their own lives. They were criminals now for having tried to overthrow the government.

Huge crowds of citizens stayed in the city, but they were not there to welcome Gorbachev as a returning hero. The hero of the coup, in their minds, was Boris Yeltsin. Yet in Yeltsin's mind, it had been a people's revolution. On Saturday, he and thousands of fellow Russians gathered for the funeral of the three comrades who had died in the coup. Wearing a bulletproof vest, Yeltsin offered the victims this good-bye: "Sleep well, our heroes, let the soil be your soft pillow."[9]

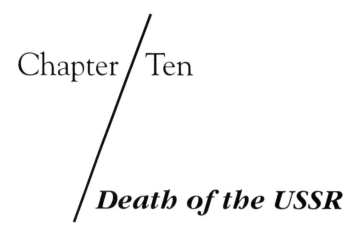

Chapter / Ten

Death of the USSR

In the days immediately after the coup, Boris Yeltsin was clearly the hero. The Russian leader had shown that he was ready to give his life for his beliefs. Mikhail Gorbachev was the badly beaten boxer who had failed to defend his title. There were many things Gorbachev could have done to make himself look better. He could have praised Boris Yeltsin for risking his life in his defense. Yet it was many days before Boris appeared on Gorbachev's "thank-you" list. It was the same with the Russian people; he made no public speeches thanking them for their support.

In fact, it seemed to many that Gorbachev wasn't doing all he should to capture the coup leaders. He refused "to turn to a witch hunt," he said, to expose Party members who had plotted against him. Why? the people cried. These plotters had done something illegal. "Perhaps," suggested one reporter, Gorbachev "feared that a serious search for villains would turn up his own name." Many people honestly blamed him for having formed this "team of traitors"[1] in the first place. It was a sign of great weakness, they said, that Gorbachev had chosen these people as his trusted aides. All this talk, combined with Gorbachev's failure to act, only made Boris look better.

After several long days of soul-searching, Gorbachev at last broke his ties with the Communist Party. He resigned as General Secretary and advised the once-powerful Central Committee to disband. A new group, the State Council, was set up to run the nation. It began to look like certain death for the Communist Party, caught in the landslide of a rapidly crumbling Soviet Union. How long could the country survive? Around the world, millions of people were asking the same question.

It was truly a time of turmoil. The coup had ended with Boris carrying the ball, and he did not intend to drop it. In the weeks that followed, he moved fast and flamboyantly. But for some, it was too fast. When he ordered six Russian newspapers to stop publication, many cried that Yeltsin was no better than the iron-fisted dictators of the past. When he became bossy to Gorbachev and criticized him in public, people called him a bully and a boor.

Leaders shuddered when Yeltsin took control of property that belonged to the central government. The Soviet Union, weak as it was, had not died yet, and until it did, no other person or group had a right to its property. By moving too quickly and roughly, by grabbing too much power, Yeltsin could do the struggling democratic movement great harm, his advisers warned.

By now, the other Soviet republics were getting worried, too. "They are afraid of Yeltsin's Russia," admitted one of Boris's top aides. "A lot of republics would prefer to see Gorbachev in charge of the center."[2] Certain world leaders—President Bush among them—agreed. But Vice President Dan Quayle and others thought that Yeltsin's beliefs and goals were closer to those of the United States than were Mikhail Gorbachev's. The world would have to wait to see who came out on top.

The wait would not be long. Events were moving at lightning speed in the Soviet Union. The question on everyone's mind was whether or not the country could survive with Gorbachev's power so weakened and the Communist Party falling apart. The Ukraine, the second most populated republic of the USSR and one of the richest in farming and industry, was now moving swiftly toward independence. Yeltsin encouraged the move.

Along with independence, Boris also pushed harder than ever for private ownership of farms and businesses. He talked of a quick removal of government controls on the prices of goods. Like pulling off a bandage, Boris believed, the move would hurt less if it were done fast. Again he warned people of hard times: "It will be worse for everybody for about six months," he predicted. But after that, "the living standards of people will gradually improve."[3]

Just to insure that his plan went forward the way he wanted, Yeltsin asked the Russian parliament for more power. He wanted to do away with any law that threatened his plans to change the economy. Immediately, cries of "Dictator!" went up from several groups. But the parliament did grant his wish. The Russian President was rapidly taking more and more power away from the Soviet government and Mikhail Gorbachev.

Yeltsin's goal was to remove price controls by January 1, 1992. It was a huge and risky change for an unstable country that had been through such upheavals during the last year. But it had to happen, Boris insisted. If Russia were going to break the bonds of Communism, it had to eliminate government controls. The people and the businesses must run the economy of the country. Only the prices of basic goods like food and fuel would still be set by the government, and these for just a short time. "This is our last chance,"[4] he warned the Russian people.

Now that Yeltsin wielded such enormous power, Soviet citizens began to criticize him, just as they had Gorbachev. For six years, they had heard nothing but promises from their government. Now, with all his warnings of hard times, it looked as if Yeltsin had no more cures for the country than had Gorbachev. "The Russian people are suffering while the fools babble,"[5] griped one Russian taxi driver. Many thought Yeltsin was edging closer to becoming a dictator. He was making big decisions completely on his own, and some were turning out to be big mistakes.

Gorbachev, meanwhile, was trying desperately to hold together what few pieces remained of the USSR. In the weeks following the coup, he had come up with a new plan he called the Union Treaty. Republics would still belong to one large country, but the central government would have far less power than in the past. Gorbachev saw it as his last chance to save the union and his job, for without a country, what would he rule? If the Union Treaty failed, Gorbachev warned the world, he would resign as President.

On November 25, 1991, his plan failed. Many of the republics—among them the Ukraine—refused to sign the Union Treaty. It was clear now that Mikhail Gorbachev's importance to the Soviet Union was ending. The republics didn't need him, and they didn't want a union with one central government. Not only had Gorbachev's plan died, but the USSR was dying, too. *Time* magazine called Gorbachev "a man without a country."[6]

Still believing that the independent republics needed some common bond, Yeltsin worked furiously on his own plan for unity. His plan would create a commonwealth—a much looser type of union than Gorbachev's. The republics that chose to join this commonwealth would work together in business matters; they might even share a common military. But each would be a free and independent country with no central government controlling the group.

When Yeltsin's commonwealth plan won a landslide victory in Russia, Gorbachev knew that his days in government were over. "The main work of my life is done,"[7] the Soviet President admitted in mid-December. With his own plan dead, Gorbachev agreed not to stand in the way of the new commonwealth.

Moving ahead with bulldozer force, Yeltsin quickly claimed for Russia all of the money and remaining property belonging to the Soviet government. It was the last gasp for the world superpower. Death came to the USSR on December 22, 1991. Eleven of the former republics agreed to join Yeltsin's new commonwealth, and a 12th showed interest in joining later. The three Baltic republics preferred not to join any union but to stay completely independent.

On Christmas day, the man without a country said good-bye. In a speech televised across the nation, Mikhail Gorbachev told the Soviet people, "I cease my activities as President of the USSR."[8] With that, he signed a paper giving Boris Yeltsin control of the 27,000 nuclear warheads in the former Soviet Union. Although the new Commonwealth of Independent States would have no single president or government, it was clear that Boris Yeltsin was the strongest leader of the strongest state in the group.

The man whom many had called a bumbler and a boor, too rash and brash ever to be a statesman, was now a world leader. He might be outspoken and rough around the edges, but he was the only president ever elected by a free vote of the Russian people. He may not have displayed the polish and charm of Mikhail Gorbachev on the world stage, but he was more popular with his own people than Gorbachev had ever been.

What had turned this child of collective farmers into a world leader? Hard work and faith in his own ideas. Boris Yeltsin was a man of action. Since boyhood he had tried always to work harder than those around him. He still works seven days a

On Christmas Day 1991, Mikhail Gorbachev turned over the reins of power to Boris Yeltsin.

week, sleeping only three to four hours a night. Learning to live with exhaustion and constant stress are, he knows, part of the price he must pay for climbing to the top.

Yeltsin has always been very sensitive to criticism. Only slowly, over many years, has he learned to accept it. Still, he admits, it is very painful for him to have his character attacked. Had Boris buckled under criticism, had he allowed himself to give in to despair, he never would have made it to the top. Faith in himself—the belief that what he was doing was right even though others might not agree—kept him from giving up. That faith gave him the courage to speak his mind, no matter how savagely others might criticize him.

The criticism isn't over. As Boris Yeltsin leads his country out of Communism, he faces constant attacks on his character. Russians want a quick solution to their troubles, and until it happens they will look for someone to blame. Many are upset with sky-high prices and food shortages. The anger of the people can be measured, wrote one reporter, "in the growing number of Russians taking to the streets to protest the policies of President Boris Yeltsin."9 Just weeks after the new commonwealth was formed, Muscovites held a rally. They cried that Yeltsin was turning Russia into a country of very poor people. At the rally, anti-Yeltsin protestors far outnumbered his supporters. Many protestors were Communists who wanted a return to the old ways. The Russian President was under pressure to prove—and soon—that democracy would work. If he failed, his country would be in chaos.

Knowing that American support was very important to his struggling democracy, Yeltsin planned another trip to the United States. This would be his first official summit meeting as President of Russia. When he arrived in Washington on June 15, 1992, two important issues were on Yeltsin's mind. He and President Bush would discuss a plan to reduce the number of nuclear weapons that each country held. Boris also hoped that the United States Congress would approve a plan pledging large amounts of aid to Russia.

At the start of the meetings, Bush praised Yeltsin. "I am dealing with a good man," he said. "I am dealing with a man who has my full support."[10] Yeltsin returned the compliment, saying that the summit was possible because of "the personal trust and confidence"[11] that he and President Bush had built since the death of the USSR.

By the end of the first day of meetings, the two leaders had reached a historic agreement. Each side promised to destroy two-thirds of its nuclear warheads by the year 2003. In fact, said Yeltsin, some of the plans they discussed would "be materialized by the year 2000."[12]

"With this agreement," said President Bush— Yeltsin standing by his side in the White House rose garden—"the nuclear nightmare recedes more and more for ourselves, for our children and for our grandchildren."[13] The agreement meant that neither country would now have the power to launch a crippling nuclear attack against the other. "We shall not fight against each other," declared the Russian leader. "This is a solemn undertaking."[14] As a further show of good faith, Yeltsin ordered the huge SS-18 nuclear missiles that had long been aimed at U.S. targets to be taken off alert, "even before the arms agreement finished this week is put into effect."[15]

There was no question that Yeltsin was trying hard to work cooperatively with the U.S. Yet he went home without the financial aid he had wanted to get from Congress. Although he is still very hopeful that the United States will help, his fellow Russians are not so sure. "Yeltsin gets applause—fine," said a Russian bus driver. "But does my family get any meat for dinner? I like that American saying, 'Where's the beef?'"[16] Another Russian, head of a large planning group in Moscow said, "Too many people hold Yeltsin responsible for what has gone wrong in their daily lives."[17]

Very hard times still lie ahead for the Russian people, and their President must find ways to steer them through. As always, Yeltsin will rely on faith in himself to do what he thinks is best, even though many may not agree. Whether his decisions prove to be right or wrong, Boris has promised his people one thing above all: He will not stand still. He is committed to action, to moving ahead, to creating a democratic country in what was once the center of world Communism. He may make mistakes, but unlike many politicans, Boris Yeltsin makes no promises that he doesn't intend to keep. "After all," he says, "in the end people are judged by real achievements and concrete results . . . not by myths and rumors."[18]

Chapter Notes

Chapter 1

1. Boris Yeltsin. "Russia Will Revive," *Vital Speeches of the Day*, September 1, 1991, p. 678.
2. Boris Yeltsin. *Against the Grain* (New York: Summit Books, 1990), p. 25
3. Ibid, p. 22.
4. Anton Antonov-Ovseyenko. *The Time of Stalin: Portrait of a Tyranny* (New York: Harper & Row, 1980), p. 57.
5. Yeltsin, *Against the Grain*, p. 36.
6. Ibid, p. 37.
7. Ibid, p. 38.

Chapter 2

1. Yeltsin, *Against the Grain*, p. 54.
2. Ibid, p. 47.
3. Ibid, p. 54.
4. Ibid, p. 95.
5. Ibid, p. 97.

6. Ibid, p. 98.
7. Ibid, p. 51.
8. Ibid, p. 52.

Chapter 3

1. Yeltsin, *Against the Grain*, p. 56.
2. Ibid, p. 65.
3. Ibid, p. 62.
4. Ibid, p. 63.
5. Ibid, p. 67.
6. Ibid, p. 69.
7. Ibid, p. 82.
8. Ibid, p. 72.
9. Ibid, p. 73.
10. Ibid, p. 76.
11. Ibid, p. 82.

Chapter 4

1. Yeltsin, *Against the Grain*, p. 89.
2. Ibid, p. 109.
3. Robert G. Kaiser. *Why Gorbachev Happened* (New York: Simon & Schuster, 1991), p. 176.
4. Yeltsin, *Against the Grain*, p. 126.

5. Ibid, p. 113.
6. Ibid, p. 154.
7. Ibid, p. 145.

Chapter 5

1. Walter Laqueur. *The Long Road to Freedom* (New York: Charles Scribner's Sons, 1989), p. 256.
2. Yeltsin, *Against the Grain*, p. 15.
3. Ibid, p. 177.
4. Ibid, p. 178.
5. Ibid, p. 181.
6. Kaiser, *Why Gorbachev Happened*, p. 180.
7. Yeltsin, *Against the Grain*, p. 186.
8. Kaiser, *Why Gorbachev Happened*, p. 183.
9. William R. Doerner. "I Am Very Guilty," *Time*, November 23, 1987, p. 34.
10. Yeltsin, *Against the Grain*, p. 199.
11. Ibid, p. 200.
12. Laqueur, *The Long Road to Freedom*, p. 257.
13. Ibid.
14. Fred Coleman. "Gorbachev's Disillusioned Intellectuals," *Newsweek*, November 30, 1987, p. 37.
15. Yelstin, *Against the Grain*, p. 195.
16. Ibid, p. 204.

17. Ibid, p. 206.
18. Ibid, p. 205.

Chapter 6

1. Yeltsin, *Against the Grain*, p. 203.
2. Ibid, p. 210.
3. Ibid, p. 222.
4. Ibid, p. 232.
5. Ibid, p. 234.
6. Ibid, p. 235.
7. John Morrison. *Boris Yeltsin: From Bolshevik to Democrat* (New York: Dutton, 1991), p. 81.
8. Yeltsin, *Against the Grain*, p. 236.
9. Ibid, p. 238.
10. Ibid, p. 239.
11. Ibid, p. 132.
12. Ibid, p. 131.
13. Morrison, *Boris Yeltsin*, p. 98

Chapter 7

1. Yeltsin, *Against the Grain*, p. 249.
2. Morrison, *Boris Yeltsin*, p. 110.

3. Paul Hendrickson. "Yeltsin's Smashing Day," *Washington Post*, September 13, 1989, Style Section.
4. Yeltsin, *Against the Grain*, p. 256.
5. Ibid, p. 257.
6. Ibid, p. 261.
7. Ibid, p. 262.
8. Morrison, *Boris Yeltsin*, p. 118.
9. Kaiser, *Why Gorbachev Happened*, p. 355.

Chapter 8

1. Morrison, *Boris Yeltsin*, p. 145.
2. David Aikman. "The Man Who Rules Russia," *Time*, September 2, 1991, p. 55.
3. Rose Brady. "The Melee in Moscow," *Business Week*, March 11, 1991, p. 52.
4. Morrison, *Boris Yeltsin*, p. 234.
5. Ibid, p. 266.
6. Ibid, p. 260.
7. Valentin Yumashev. "Boris Yeltsin Explains," *World Press Review*, January 1990, p. 65.

Chapter 9

1. Morrison, *Boris Yeltsin*, p. 275.

2. Lawrence Elliott & David Satter. "Three Days That Shook the World," *Reader's Digest*, January 1992, p. 63.
3. Ibid, p. 183.
4. Ibid, p. 191.
5. Ibid, p. 187.
6. George J. Church. "Anatomy of a Coup," *Time*, September 2, 1991, p. 38.
7. Michael Ryan & Maria Wilhelm. "Standing Tall," *People*, September 9, 1991, p. 39.
8. Ibid, p. 40.
9. Rae Corelli. "Red Is Dead," *Maclean's*, September 2, 1991, p. 29.

Chapter 10

1. Bruce W. Nelan. "Desperate Moves," *Time*, September 2, 1991, p. 27.
2. Russell Watson. "End of an Empire," *Newsweek*, September 9, 1991, p. 19.
3. Associated Press. "Yeltsin Offers Russia Painful Road to Economic Reform," *Rocky Mountain News*, October 29, 1991, p. 3.
4. Holger Jensen. "Cabbie's Telltale Lament," *Rocky Mountain News*, November 24, 1991, p. 3.
5. Ibid.
6. *Time*, December 23, 1991, cover.

7. Associated Press. "Gorbachev Nears Resignation," *Rocky Mountain News*, December 13, 1991, p. 3.

8. Associated Press. "Gorbachev Takes Final Bow," *Rocky Mountain News*, December 26, 1991, p. 3.

9. Holger Jensen. "Hungry Russians Are Only a Half Step From Revolution," *Rocky Mountain News*, February 11, 1992, p. 3.

10. Mark Matthews. "Bush, Yeltsin betting on success," *Denver Post*. June 16, 1992, p. 2A.

11. Denver Post Wire Services. "Warheads limited to 3,500 each," *Denver Post*, June 17, 1992, p. 1A

12. Reuters News Service. "Excerpts From Bush-Yeltsin Conference: Working Toward a Safer World," The *New York Times*, June 17, 1992, p. A7.

13. Denver Post Wire Services. "Warheads limited to 3,500 each," *Denver Post*, June, 1992, p. 1A.

14. Ibid.

15. "Yeltsin Pledges to Block Any Efforts to Roll Back Russian Economic Reforms," *Wall Street Journal*, June 18, 1992 p. A18.

16. Michael Parks. "Russian gets mixed reviews back home," *Denver Post*, June 19, 1992. p. 9A.

17. Ibid.

18. Yeltsin, *Against the Grain*, p. 260

Appendix One
A Glossary of
Special Terms

Apparat—A group of full-time bureaucrats, faithful members of the Communist Party.

Central Committee—A group of approximately 400 top members elected from the Communist Party Congress. Met twice a year to write proposals that would be passed on to the Politburo for approval. Yeltsin was once head of construction on the Central Committee in Moscow. This was a Party position, not a government post.

City Committee—A local group of Communist Party members within a city. In Moscow, the City Committee had 1.2 million members. Yeltsin replaced Viktor Grishin as chairman or head of the Moscow City Committee in 1985. The committee was made up of Party members, not government officials.

Collectivism—A political/economic system used in many Communist countries. Under collectivism, the government controls production and distribution of goods. Collective farms are one example of collectivism.

Commonwealth of Independent States—Name for 11 of the republics thar once made up the USSR. Members are independent republics ruled by their own governments rather than by one central government. The CIS was formed early in 1992 on a plan developed by Boris Yeltsin after the death of the Soviet Union.

Communist Party—The only political party allowed in Communist countries, made up of people who believe in the principles of Communism. Technically the Party is separate from the government, but in truth, Party members control the actions of the government. In the USSR there were Communist Party groups at all levels, from factories and universities, to cities, provinces, and republics.

Communist Party Congress—Meetings of delegates from the Communist Party that took place once every five years. From this group, the Central Committee was chosen, which met twice a year.

Congress of People's Deputies—Created after changes were made in the structure of Soviet government in 1988. The Congress consisted of 2,250 deputies elected from around the country. It met once a year to discuss issues related to lawmaking. The upper house of the Congress was the Supreme Soviet. The Congress was a government body, not a Party organization.

First Secretary (of a province)—The most powerful person in a Soviet province, a region roughly similar to a state in the United States. Both Gorbachev and Yeltsin were First Secretaries from their provinces—Stavropol and Sverdlovsk. This was a Party position, not a governmental post.

General Secretary of the Communist Party—The chief member of the Central Committee and the most powerful position in the Communist Party. Gorbachev became General Secretary in 1985.

Glasnost—A policy of "greater openness" in the USSR. *Glasnost* allowed people to speak their minds or write their opinions in newspapers and magazines without fear of being punished by the Communist Party. Yeltsin was a great supporter of *glasnost*.

IRGD: Inter-Regional Group of Deputies—A subgroup within the Congress of People's Deputies started in 1989 by Yeltsin and his fellow radicals ,who were trying to make their ideas for reform heard in the Soviet Union.

KGB—Abbreviation for Komitet Gosudarstvennoy Bezopasnosti, in English "Committee of State Security." This was the police and intelligence agency of the former Soviet Union.

Party Conference—A periodic meeting of nearly 5,000 people selected from within the Communist Party. Members represented all the Soviet republics and other Communist countries elsewhere in the world. This was a smaller, regional meeting of Communist Party members that took place before the Party Congresses.

Perestroika—Gorbachev's plan for restructuring the economy and politics of the USSR. Gorbachev made great strides in political reform, but Yeltsin was impatient with the pace at which economic restructuring took place.

Plenum—A meeting of Communist Party committees at any level, from local to national, but usually refers to a meeting of the Central Committee.

Politburo—(Short for Political Bureau) A select group of 15 to 20 members, chosen by Party leaders from the Central Committee to act for the Party when the Congress was not in session. Met once or twice a week to make decisions for the USSR. This was the real center of power in the Soviet Union. The country's most important leaders belonged to the Politburo.

Soviet Union—Shortened form of the Union of Soviet Socialist Republics (USSR), once the largest country in the world. It was formed in 1922 with four republics and grew to fifteen before its breakup in 1991.

Supreme Soviet—The upper house of the Congress of People's Deputies, made up of 542 members elected from the Congress who were responsible for making laws in the USSR. The Supreme Soviet met twice a year for three or four months. It elected the president of the USSR, the last president being Gorbachev.

Appendix Two
Boris Yeltsin:
A Time Line

February 1, 1931—Boris Nikolayevich Yeltsin (or El'tsin) born in Butko, Sverdlovsk Province, Russian Republic, USSR.

1955—Graduates from Urals Polytechnic Institute, where he studied civil engineering.

1956—Marries Naya Girina of Orenburg Province, whom he met while both were students at the Polytechnic.

1957—Daughter Lena born. Like her father, she would later study civil engineering at Urals Polytechnic.

1959—Daughter Tanya born. Tanya would later study mathematics and cybernetics—the relation between the brain and the automatic control of machines—at Moscow University.

1961—Yeltsin joins the Communist Party.

1969—Yeltsin becomes a full-time Communist Party official, responsible for all construction in Sverdlovsk Province.

1976—Becomes First Secretary of Sverdlovsk Province, a step up the ladder in the Communist Party. His rank is now equal to that of Mikhail Gorbachev, who is First Secretary in Stavropol Province. Yeltsin will hold the post for nine years.

1981—Yeltsin elected to Central Committee of the Communist Party, a "rubber-stamp" group that meets only twice a year for two or three hours.

March 1985—Mikhail Gorbachev becomes General Secretary of the Central Committee, the highest position in the Communist Party.

April 12, 1985—Yeltsin moves to Moscow to become head of construction for the Central Committee. Two months later, becomes a Central Committee Secretary.

December 24, 1985—Becomes chairman of the Moscow City Committee of the Communist Party.

February 18, 1986—Chosen as a candidate member of the Politburo, the real center of power in the Communist Party.

September 12, 1987—Boris Yeltsin writes letter of resignation to Mikhail Gorbachev, asking to be removed from his position in the Politburo and the Moscow City Committee.

October 21, 1987—At a plenum of the Central Committee, Yeltsin asks to be relieved of his duties. Criticizes Party leaders for inaction. His speech is followed by verbal attacks against him from other committee members in what would become known as the Yeltsin Affair.

November 11, 1987—Yeltsin called from his hospital bed to attend a meeting of the Moscow City Committee, where he is slaughtered politically by other Party members. In the end, the Committee accepts his resignation. Surprisingly, just days later, Gorbachev offers him post of First Deputy Chairman of the State Committee for Construction. Yeltsin accepts.

June 1988—Public rallies to Yeltsin's defense after attacks against him at the Nineteenth Party Conference.

March 26, 1989—In the first free elections since 1917, Yeltsin is voted into the Congress of People's Deputies, winning 89.6 percent of the vote.

May 25, 1989—Mikhail Gorbachev becomes President of the USSR.

June–July 1989—The IRGD, a subgroup in Congress started by Yeltsin and his fellow radicals, gains an increasingly strong voice in the Supreme Soviet.

September 1989—Yeltsin visits the United States. His trip is haunted by reports of drunkenness and excessive spending, which he strongly denies.

May 1990—Yeltsin elected to lead the Russian parliament, becoming chairman of the Russian Supreme Soviet (a position in the Russian Republic, not the USSR).

July 1990—At a meeting of the Twenty-eighth Party Congress, Yeltsin announces his decision to quit the Communist Party. His move shocks the nation.

January 1991—Violence erupts in the three Baltic republics of the USSR. The issue is independence for the republics.

June 12, 1991—Boris Yeltsin becomes the first President of the Russian Republic to be elected directly by the people, winning more than half the vote.

July 1991—Visits the United States, this time to a better reception and a meeting with President George Bush.

August 1991—Becomes a hero when, with the support of the Russian people, he overthrows a coup attempt by hard-line Communists.

December 22, 1991—Death comes to the Soviet Union when 11 former republics agree to join Yeltsin's new commonwealth. Three days later, Gorbachev resigns as President of the USSR.

January 2, 1992—Yeltsin removes government controls on prices of goods. Prices soar. New challenges face the Russian people.

June 15, 1992—Yeltsin travels to the United States for his first summit meeting as President of Russia. On June 15, he and President Bush reach a historic agreement. Each country promises to reduce the number of its nuclear warheads to 3,500 by the year 2003. "We shall not fight against each other," Yeltsin declares.

Selected Bibliography

Books

Hart, Gary. *Russia Shakes the World*. New York: Harper-Collins, 1991.

Kaiser, Robert G. *Why Gorbachev Happened*. New York: Simon & Schuster, 1991.

Laqueur, Walter. *The Long Road to Freedom*. New York: Charles Scribner's Sons, 1989.

Morrison, John. *Boris Yeltsin: From Bolshevik to Democrat*. New York: Penguin Books, 1991.

Oleksy, Walter. *Mikhail Gorbachev: A Leader for Soviet Change*. Chicago: Childrens Press, 1989.

Resnick, Abraham. *Enchantment of the World: The Union of Soviet Socialist Republics*. Chicago: Regensteiner Publishing, 1989.

Yeltsin, Boris. *Against the Grain*. New York: Summit Books, 1990.

News Magazines

Business Week, March 11, 1991, p. 52; April 1, 1991, pp. 38–39; June 24, 1991, pp. 56–57; September 2, 1991, pp. 20–26.

Maclean's, September 2, 1991, pp. 22–23, 24–29, 32–33, 44; June 24, 1991, pp. 36–37.

Newsweek, November 30, 1987, p. 37; June 13, 1988, p. 23; June 11, 1990, pp. 20–25; June 24, 1991, pp. 28–31; September 2, 1991, pp. 46–48; September 9, 1991, pp. 18–23.

Scholastic Update, December 7, 1990.

Time, November 23, 1987, p. 34; September 22, 1991, pp. 20–23, 24–28, 33–44, 48, 49, 54–55; December 23, 1991, pp. 18–22, 24–27.

U.S. News & World Report, March 28, 1988, pp. 30–33; April 8, 1991, pp. 38–40, 43; March 25, 1991, pp. 33–34; June 17, 1991, pp. 36–38; September 2, 1991, pp. 26–38, 38–41; September 9, 1991, pp. 20–30, 32.

Periodicals

Elliott, Lawrence, and Satter, David. "Three Days That Shook the World." *Reader's Digest*, January 1992, p. 60+.

Evans, Rowland, and Novak, Robert. "Is Boris Yeltsin for Real?" *Reader's Digest*, July 1991, pp. 45–49.

Ryan, Michael, and Wilhelm, Maria. "Standing Tall." *People*, September 9, 1991, pp. 38–43.

Keller, Bill. "Boris Yeltsin Taking Power." *New York Times Magazine*, September 23, 1990, p. 33+.

Yeltsin, Boris. "Russia Will Revive." *Vital Speeches of the Day*, September 1, 1991, pp. 677–678.

Index